THE
POLICE TRAINING OFFICER

The

Police Training Officer

By

DAVID A. HANSEN
Supervising Captain
Daly City Police Department

THOMAS R. CULLEY
Lieutenant, Patrol Division
Daly City Police Department

With a Foreword by

S. I. Hayakawa
President
California State University
San Francisco, California
formerly
San Francisco State College

Illustrations by

John Richardson
Officer
California Highway Patrol

CHARLES C THOMAS · PUBLISHER
Springfield · Illinois · U.S.A.

Published and Distributed Throughout the World by
CHARLES C THOMAS • PUBLISHER
BANNERSTONE HOUSE
301-327 East Lawrence Avenue, Springfield, Illinois, U.S.A.

© *1973, by* CHARLES C THOMAS • PUBLISHER
ISBN 0-398-02493-6
Library of Congress Catalog Card Number: 73-190324

Printed in the United States of America
N-1

We dedicate this book to all trainers with the desire to teach and the guts to make their programs work. We also offer a special salute to P.O.S.T. and all similar organizations dedicated to police profession- alization through training.

ACKNOWLEDGMENTS

W<small>E GRATEFULLY ACKNOWLEDGE</small> the assistance and inspiration of Chief Roland Petrocchi, Daly City Police Department, the Training Division, and all whose efforts have made our program what it is today.

FOREWORD

Daly City is a suburban city of some seventy thousand population, lying immediately south of San Francisco, so that its borders are within a few blocks of San Francisco State College. Many of the faculty and students live in Daly City, so that there has long been a cordial relationship between the town and the college.

During the dreadful academic year of 1968-69, when radical dissidents attempted to close down San Francisco State College, by disruption to make instruction impossible and by violence and threats of violence to keep nonstriking faculty and students from attending classes, an especially close tie was created between Daly City and the college. Daly City police, along with police from other cities in the Bay Area, served with the San Francisco Police Department under mutual aid agreements to help restore order to our beleaguered campus.

At the height of the uproar in December 1968 and January 1969, as many as six hundred officers were on campus on some days, including sixty-five from the Daly City Police Department. The success of the police in containing the uproar, protecting students and faculty and stopping the disruption of campus activities was the most important factor in restoring peace—and education —to the campus of San Francisco State.

Incidentally, some of the officers—especially among those from Daly City and San Francisco—performed in a double capacity during this period. When police duties were done, they ran home and changed clothes to return to the campus as students. The school they were saving was their own.

It is a great pleasure for me, therefore, because of past events as well as continuing neighborly relations and common interests, to commend to the attention of the law enforcement profession *The Police Training Officer* by Captain David A. Hansen and

Lieutenant Thomas R. Culley of the Daly City Police Department. In their previous book, *The Police Leader*, the authors proved themselves leaders of police leaders. The present book proves them educators of police educators. Their book shows experienced insight into the problems of those responsible for the education and training of others—what to look for in one's self as well as in one's trainees that will prove to be problems—and how to face such problems. Their deep concern with adequacy and accuracy of communication both within departments and between departments is in harmony with trends in both business management and public service, in which there is increasing awareness of the degree to which failures of communication affect individuals and groups at all levels of complex organizations.

Finally throughout the book the reader will find unobtrusive but clear evidence of the moral and ethical problems involved in law enforcement; in the problems of personnel evaluation; in the relations of superior to subordinate, of trainer to trainee, of interrrogating officer to suspects or witnesses. In short, *The Police Training Officer*, in addition to being a substantial contribution to police professionalism, is a wise book.

S. I. HAYAKAWA

INTRODUCTION

W E DO NOT believe there is a police administrator anywhere who will not acknowledge that training is an important factor in the makeup of his department. It is unfortunate that many of these same administrators are dreadfully shortsighted in selecting their training officer and then overseeing his training.

It is common for the administrator to call in his "good supervisor" or officer and make him training officer. By making his proclamation and handing down the title, the Chief may now step aside, and the training officer will take over.

It is a nice dream, but there is much more to the making of a training officer than application of the title. To perform with any effectiveness at all, the man must first be prepared to do the job. He must understand the mechanics of preparing material, delivering the message and evaluating the results. In short, he must be a teacher.

In this writing the authors propose to offer distinct guidelines for selection of the training officer and other instructors, and suggestions for building his qualifications for the job.

We believe that a properly prepared trainer can produce a well-trained officer, and a poorly trained instructor can possibly ruin an otherwise good man. We also believe that there is more to consider than years of experience and education in selecting a trainer. Obviously those are important factors, but equally important are the abilities to communicate and determine how well the message is being received.

We will discuss methods of planning various training programs and exercises and the value of interdepartmental programs. We will also uncover some of the pitfalls in such programs.

It is our belief that a training program must be equal to the men to be trained. A program that lingers too long on simple basics in class may become tiresome and as one educator once put it: "The brain will absorb only as much as the bottom can bear." We emphasize the value of mixing class time with field or gym activities in lengthy programs, both for the physical activitiy it gives the men, and the opportunity it provides to apply what they have learned.

Included in our writings are suggested schedules of instruction for recruits as well as material related to advanced training for experienced personnel and supervisors. We believe that training is an endless process and no man in the police field ever knows everything.

Experience has taught us the value of television in "roll call" training, when the time is limited, and there is need to deliver a message uniformly to all hands. By using this medium the same message by the same instructor is given to all.

Encompassed in this book are sample lesson plans of varying length, designed to show how some material might be presented. We also have included a list of words commonly used in police reports and commonly misspelled by policemen.

In our chapter on "Report Writing," we comment on the need for accuracy in spelling as well as in report content. We also demonstrate a report system adopted by the Daly City Police Department several years ago that provides a means of locating specifics within the report with minimum searching.

Throughout this book we will stress the importance of maintaining proper discipline in all training situations. We cite this because discipline in training is at the heart of the matter. A student who is not compelled to maintain a notebook or to account in any way for his having learned the lessons will soon find his interests wandering. If the instructor thinks so little of his subject and his students that he fails to require some effort on their part and some proof of that effort he has failed his students.

In no business are the changes so radical and so sudden as in the field of law enforcement. Court decisions are handed down, lawmaking bodies drastically change laws, and the public demand for specific types of service must be met and dealt with. All of these factors, along with the sociological changes within our country, make flexibility of training an absolute necessity.

We have chosen to go beyond the basic thought of training an effective patrol force. We strongly believe that when we ask a man to perform any job, we must first train him to carry out that task. For this reason we have attempted to cover some other areas of police work, such as assignments in detective work and communications.

We also know that as men prepare to advance they must be properly trained in the techniques and responsibilities necessary in the new position.

In most civil service examinations for promotions, many questions are asked concerning supervision and administration and other areas in which the supervisor must function. Almost without exception the candidates must seek out this information on their own, relying often on outdated, largely opinionated writings.

We have emphasized in our department the role that each supervisor must play in preparing his subordinates for future promotions. It is indeed a comment on the ability and attitude of a supervisor whose men frequently place well on promotional examinations.

It is also a comment on the efficiency of a department and its training program when promotions come from within and the jobs are filled with superior personnel.

We have noted that the reputation of a department with a solid training program seems to grow constantly, and the department is held in high esteem by colleagues and citizenry.

We cannot claim that we have all of the answers to training problems that relate to your department, nor can we presume to set ourselves apart as "experts." We do respectfully offer our thoughts and our successes in the firm belief that what has worked for us will work for others.

CONTENTS

PART V
TRAINING FOR PROMOTION AND SUPERVISORS

THE
POLICE TRAINING OFFICER

PART I
THE TRAINING OFFICER

Chapter 1

SELECTING AND TRAINING THE TRAINING OFFICER

I N TODAY's modern police departments, the emphasis is on training to develop a highly skilled, efficiently operated organization. At the root of this training is the training officer.

For many years it was policy for police departments to hire a man and train him by letting him ride with a veteran officer for a week or two and then send him out to do the job. Many men worked hard and became fine officers in spite of this poor beginning. Many others floundered or became discouraged and left the field.

Today, with the multitude of laws and court decisions that must be interpreted and applied in the daily work of the policeman, as well as the state of social turmoil that exists in our society, in order to survive and provide any kind of effective protection to the citizens, an officer must be thoroughly trained in a wide variety of subjects.

The true test of the effectiveness of a police department is meeting the needs of the community, and carrying cases through to successful prosecution. We submit that the department with a sound training platform will meet the needs of the community and provide the public with officers who are well prepared to carry out the role of investigator to successful prosecution.

In small departments with only a few men, the training may be carried on by supervisors, or perhaps the Chief himself will train his personnel. In many cases officers are sent to larger cities to attend academy training, or perhaps to a program conducted through a community college. We commend such programs. Police academies that provide services for a number of departments offer more than the lessons of the classroom. They offer an opportunity for the recruit to make contacts with officers of neighboring departments, and to learn first-hand about the vari-

"I'll teach them all I know."

ous problems facing people in other departments. Generally schools of this kind are staffed by experienced officers and professionals in related fields who offer a wide range of knowledge and experience to the recruits. For many of the instructors, teaching in classes of this kind is their way of contributing their effort toward more professional and competent police officers. We know of no instructors who do not find the experience rewarding.

Training in an academy or community college setting is good, but by no means can such a program offer or produce a completely trained officer. Each department has rules and regulations and each jurisdiction is subject to policies and practices that will differ slightly from others. It is therefore necessary to conduct classes and field training programs for recruits to make them familiar with such rules and policies.

Toward this end, it is important that the responsibility for training be clearly designated. A training officer or division must be provided, and they must be adequate for the job.

We submit that in making selections in this area, the administrator must consider a number of factors. One factor is motivation. A man who likes to work on the street and take a strong active part in investigations may have an intense dislike for the atmosphere of the classroom, and therefore be a poor teacher. The administrator should review the background and interests of his personnel and seek out those who have shown a strong interest in training or teaching. The man who has obtained a teaching credential and teaches in a police academy, or community college has displayed an obvious interest, and may be a good choice, if in the eyes of the Chief he is otherwise qualified.

Generally a training officer should be someone of supervisory rank, preferably a sergeant. We feel a sergeant is the most desireable rank because he is close to the men and can relate to them easily, yet he has the authority and the demonstrated ability behind him.

It is a mistake for the selection to be made based only on the fact the man is a "good supervisor." Often a man who is a fine street supervisor is lost within the classroom and unfamiliar with the need for scheduling classes within the program, and the techniques of teaching. Too often a good sergeant might be lost in the training slot because of inadequate preparation. It is as important to train the training officer as it is to train the men, if not more important.

Toward this end there are a number of suggested courses of action that might be followed. One course would be programs within the community college system, or university, whereby the man could obtain professional instruction in the techniques of teaching. Such programs often lead to issuance of a credential to teach in the field.

Another possible method of training would be to visit an established academy or school and observe the techniques employed by the instructors for a period.

Whatever method is selected, the administrator should observe the trainer in action for a time and evaluate the results of the training himself, or through his designate.

Throughout training progress reports should be submitted on each trainee and maintained as part of his permanent record, and a summation of these progress reports should be kept in a file on the trainer.

If more than one person is assigned to training, the administrator must evaluate the selections carefully and establish clear-cut lines of authority and responsibility to report to the office of the Chief.

The officer in charge of the training detail should have broad knowledge and experience in the field so that he can oversee the other instructors as they perform. Each instructor should be required to develop his plans for teaching his subject under this supervision.

In considering persons as potential instructors the administrator should capitalize on the expertise of his instructors and allow them to teach in areas in which they specialize or have some specific interest or experience. A man is most comfortable and usually most capable teaching in his specialty.

Some instructors may be called upon on a part-time basis only. Care must be taken to insure that they are allowed sufficient time to prepare or update lesson materials to be presented well in advance of the actual teaching day. In addition to submitting lesson plans, the instructors should also be asked to prepare questions for an examination on their subjects.

By requiring each instructor to submit lesson plans for the topics they teach, it is possible to build an excellent training manual or file for future use. A well-prepared lesson plan could then be passed on to another instructor in the future, should the need arise.

In addition to the lesson plans submitted by the instructors, the training officer should also accumulate books, articles, bulletins and other material to be placed in the training files against future use.

Tape recordings, motion pictures and video-tapes are also excellent assets within such a file.

We feel it advisable at this point to suggest that controls over the use of the training file be stringently enforced, lest the wealth of material somehow disappear.

When preparing lessons for the training file, it is wise to prepare them with duplication in mind, by putting them on mimeograph stencils or similar material in order that they can be reproduced as many times as desired. In the chapter on "Lesson Plans" we will discuss the training files in more depth.

Another factor that the administrator should consider in making selections of training officers is their appearance. A man who looks neat, clean and in generally good physical condition obviously makes a better impression on the class and commands attention. The man who is sloppy or careless in his appearance loses something of his emphasis as a leader. By no means do we imply that appearance would be the only basis for selection. A good looking man who cannot deliver as a teacher, and the fat or sloppy man who is a good teacher cannot be compared. Obviously it is best to choose the best teacher and sacrifice the appearance aspect.

If the class is to be taught to police officers, generally it is best to have the trainer in uniform. If their role is to be carried out in a field exercise or gymnasium, the trainer should be garbed in appropriate clothing for the situation.

It goes without saying that the administrator will select trainers who are loyal to him and the department. We feel that the man must be more than loyal. He must be a booster of the department, working to impress on the minds of his charges the benefits to be derived from diligent performance of their duties, and the loyalty that the department will show to them in so many ways.

We do not wish to suggest that the man should spend all his time waving flags and giving speeches. We do suggest that a strong positive approach on the part of the trainer will influence the attitude of the recruit, and perhaps help him to avoid the pitfalls of some morale problems over the years.

We know that a good teacher must be constantly updating his lesson material to keep abreast of the changing times. Such changing can only be accomplished by spending a good deal of time reading, attending lectures and classes, and seeking out the information that is available in the field. This is generally accomplished in off-duty time and effort. Therefore when a training officer is selected, such initiative on his part is a factor that must be considered. A man who tries to get by with the minimum effort at all times will probably not be able to instill those qualities in the minds of others that create initiative.

We cannot expect that all students will adopt the policies or attitudes of their teacher. We should strive to give them the benefit of the best possible leader to emulate.

The authors feel that recognition for a job well done is important, and good or outstanding performance by a recruit or trainee should be given proper notice and attention. The trainer must not be forgotten at this time. If the men succeed, often it will be because he has done a good job in preparing them. It is our feeling that such performance should not go unnoticed.

We do not suggest that a formal commendation is due a man who performs the work he is expected to carry out. We do feel that a high grade on an evaluation report, or a favorable comment in the personnel jacket are in order when the man is deserving. Most policemen find the role of teacher tame and unexciting in comparison to being on the street. To give them some measure of recognition for their work will make that work much more pleasurable.

We speak from experience when we say it is a very rewarding moment when a man we have trained performs an outstanding job, or receives an award for exemplary performance of his duties. We can privately share in the pride he feels, knowing we had at least a part in helping to bring it about.

Preparing and motivating your training officer are as important to a successful program as conception and pregnancy are to childbirth.

We previously mentioned that there are programs of various types offered in community colleges and universities. This kind of professional training can be very important because it will provide the formal techniques of teaching and testing that are essential to know.

It may be that your candidate has already had some formal training, and in that case you can be selective about what formal classes he will attend. Perhaps classes on the use of visual aids and preparation of video-tapes would be of benefit.

Courses in psychology that relate to education may open some avenues that might otherwise be missed. It is found that courses of this sort can be invaluable to the instructor who is faced with some opposition or hesitancy on the part of his students.

Courses dealing with some specific areas of law enforcement can also be important. By keeping current with new techniques or attitudes the officer is more effective and a better teacher.

When the need for training is obvious, the administrator is often in a hurry to get started. We feel he must withhold starting a program until his instructor (s) can be properly prepared. To expect men to learn from a person who does not have the ability to reach them, or the knowledge necessary to train them, is to court disaster.

We suggest that a Chief who wishes to establish a training division can get many ideas from neighboring departments where established programs already exist. In the same manner he might also obtain some training for his instructors by allowing them to observe the program in action for a period.

Another source of advice and guidance can be a community college. Perhaps the head of the Criminology or Police Science Department can assist and advise in establishing a program and training the instructors.

The State Department of Education can give information concerning the requirements for credentials, and often can provide a wealth of training materials at very low cost.

There are many writings on the subject of adult education and there is much to be learned from such sources about the mechanics of preparation of lessons, course planning and selection of materials.

You would not send a man to court to prosecute a case without preparation. You cannot send a man to train others without training.

We will offer in these writings some particular suggestions concerning police officers. We do not presume to offer our work as the total answer to establishing a training division.

Chapter 2

THE MISSION OF THE
TRAINING OFFICER

IN THE FIRST chapter we touched a little on the mission of the training officer when we spoke of the attitude and initiative he will hope to bring about in his charges. In this chapter we will put forth some ideas of the goals we hope to achieve by appointing a training officer or division.

The primary and obvious mission of the training officer is to bring all of the policemen in his department to a point of maximum knowledge and proficiency, with as little interruption of their work function as possible.

To the training officer will fall the responsibility of creating police officers from raw recruits. He will be expected to groom them to function smoothly under stress and with sufficient knowledge to serve the public capably.

As laws are passed and changes come about through legislation and court decision, the training officer will find himself with the duty of disseminating the information to all concerned persons within the department.

In this role, he will learn the intricate language of the "legal types," who seem bent on warping the mind of the reader with each sentence. He will also learn the value of his district attorney to act as an interpreter and to offer opinions concerning laws and decisions. His mission here is to prevent error that might result from misinterpretation of the law and perhaps serious results for the offender and the officer alike.

It might be said that the training officer has the mission of stimulating minds that have often gone undisturbed by formal education for long periods. He may also find some resentment from officers of similar rank or experience as he drills them in their lessons. We will comment further in a later chapter on the problems of in-service programs.

13

"Train the new man."

A mission of the training officer we feel is very important, and often neglected, is that of creating training programs that are new or not adequately covered in the existing training schedule of a department.

There are many fields, not directly related to police work, from which the police can learn a great deal. Certain areas of public relations, community relations and personnel management are handled in a very sophisticated manner by businesses. Police agencies unfortunately are still struggling in these areas, and have often failed to look about at what industry has done in the same areas. We submit that a training program might well be adapted from industry that could fill such gaps and by pursuing such a course the training officer is doing his organization a great service.

"Now I want you guys to get this right."

By no means do we limit such thinking to the suggested programs. We are certain that by exchanging ideas with other police agencies, colleges, and others, the training officer will uncover programs that will benefit his department a great deal.

The basic mission seems so simple and logical that one may question why this chapter need be written. The authors feel that all too often the mission is subverted by failure to provide ample time, manpower, and equipment to the training officer. He must be free of this kind of worry to do the job well.

If the mission is to train the people, the Chief must allow the man access to the people. He must arrange a time and place for training to take place.

It is a fallacy to think that having a bulletin prepared to be read to, or by, the men at roll call will really do the job of training them. Of course it is possible to inform them of some procedures or changes in this manner, but it is a poor way to carry out any involved training.

An example of a program requiring such provision is training for riot control. You cannot tell the men how to get into formations and expect them to function. They must work together and move through the formations walking and then running so they come to move together and operate as a well-drilled unit.

It is very unfortunate that in many departments training takes a back seat. The need for formal training goes unacknowledged and the men are sent out to do a job without proper preparation. It is not until a serious mistake is made, or some public criticism comes about that the administrator realizes the inadequacy of his programs.

Just as it is the mission of the training division to keep the men informed, it is also the mission of the training division to keep the Chief informed what is going on. As information comes to the training division concerning new programs, or new equipment adopted for police work, the Chief should be informed and all possible information given him concerning the value to the department. Often a Chief will already have some information through publications or other contacts, but without detailed information he may not realize the value or application to his department.

It may seem that we are telling the training officer to train his Chief. This is not really far from wrong. We do not suggest that there is anything lacking in the administrators. We do suggest that any busy executive will find himself hard pressed to personally investigate everything that comes up. If he can rely on his aide to carry out this function and report to him, he is relieved of a time-consuming duty and his department may benefit where otherwise it would not.

There is a danger that we must mention, and that is the training officer who gets himself too entangled in looking at other peoples' programs and neglects his own duties. It would be foolish, for example, for the training officer from a sixty man department to spend time learning the techniques of scheduling classes for hundreds of men.

It is also possible for the training officer to lose a great deal of time viewing equipment and listening to salesmen. He must be careful to concern himself with such equipment that seems to fill some need within his department.

There is a subtle mission of the training division, and that is maintaining the desire to learn and improve in officers at all levels of experience. We describe this as subtle because, while real and important, it is seldom announced as a part of the program.

This is a very difficult, if not impossible mission. Many officers will lose initiative simply because they stagnate in their jobs. To stimulate some of these men is difficult indeed. We must try nevertheless.

One very important mission of the training division is to help the economy of the department. By this we mean that by providing a high level of training and proficiency, the officers can work more effectively with less direct supervision.

Effective enforcement policies result in more fines levied and less cost to the citizens from crime and accidents, a very positive element indeed when we are seeking public support for our programs.

Chapter 3

EVALUATING THE TRAINING PROGRAM

Training practices must, for a number of reasons, be continuously measured and evaluated. The conducting of training is worthless, and perhaps even counterproductive, unless we are able to accomplish the goals of that training.

This is determined by an evaluation of that training. Without a viable and realistic evaluation, any conclusion which we might make is only guesswork. Guesswork, in training as in all of police work, is haphazard and inefficient; it is a waste of time and effort inasmuch as it does not result in a true picture.

Plans need to be formulated for further training. Such additional training must be connected to, proceed from, and add to the initial training. We will not know where to begin the additional training if we are unable to discern what has been accomplished thus far. We cannot tell where we are going, or even what direction should be taken, unless we know where it is that we have been.

In our evaluation we must determine the effectiveness of the instructor. This has to be a continuing process, and often we must be somewhat heartless about it. If the deficient instructor can be, himself, retrained and/or counseled, and thus salvaged, then this should be done. Short of that possibility, or perhaps probability, then the instructor must be replaced.

For example, the instructor who is thought of as a "nice guy" by his class is not necessarily a competent instructor. Many a marginal instructor will endeavor to woo his class by the telling of "sea stories." Stories, examples, are good for illustrative purposes, without doubt; a class consisting of gossip and fairy tales does not supplant the need for theory, however entertaining it may, or may not, be to the students.

The instructor who "passes" all of his students is not necessarily a competent instructor. He may be competent, but evaluation

"Hmmmm—I didn't know that."

of him should certainly take into consideration this aspect of his character. He may be incapable of failing a student; he is not doing the marginal student any favors by passing him along. Future supervisors of such students will resoundly curse this trainer, and with good cause. The marginal student is a marginal, and often worse, officer.

The instructor who fails all of his students is definitely a failure as an instructor. An instructor exists to teach students. If all or most of his students fail to learn, then both they and the instructor are failures. Such an instructor usually lacks the realities of a good street policeman, and of course cannot pass on those realities to his students. The instructor must be replaced.

Unsigned student critique sheets should be implemented and *utilized* for and about each instructor. Granted, an occasional disgruntled student will maliciously malign a tough instructor; most students will appreciate a tough instructor. Such critiques must be reviewed. Instructors should be appraised of the critiques. Proper counseling of the instructor should accompany the formal critique session between the instructor and his supervisor.

An occasional visit to a place and period of instruction will afford the training officer an opportunity to make a firsthand evaluation of the instructor, the subject matter, and the class. While this can be overdone, and can create a harrassment of the instructor, in some moderation it is a valuable technique. The technique tends to keep the instructor "honest."

These methods form a base from which instruction can be strengthened. Subject matter must consistently be upgraded and updated. Instruction must be of *this* year's court decisions, and about *today's* methods.

The subject matter can be improved by class visits by the trainer, who acts from his observations. The perusal of the student critiques will assist in evaluating whether and how much the instructor was getting across to the students. Checking testing results will assist the trainer in finding how well the material is being received by the students.

We also have to determine whether the instruction meets the needs of the men. Is it, in fact, relevant? If theory and "how to do" instruction does not square with the cold world of street police work, great harm is done to the department. When this occurs, not only have the instructor and students wasted their time, but line supervisors are burdened with partly trained men on the street. The department as a whole suffers. Retraining on the street becomes necessary.

A further word, however, about "retraining." The training officer, as we suggest elsewhere in these writings, hopefully has good liaison and rapport with his line supervisor counterparts. We say "hopefully"; though it is not universal, it is essential. The training officer must be able to balance instructional material with street needs. He must insist that the two equate. He satisfies himself of this by random sampling of line supervisor opinion and by observation on the street. Do his "good" students become good street officers? Some record keeping is necessary here.

Once the training officer determines that his training is valid and relevant, then he should take a hard look at the line supervisors. How often this?: "OK, kid, you're out of the Academy now. Now I'll show you how we really do it." Too, too often.

This occurs when instruction is irrelevent, or at least unrealistic. Our trainer has already either corrected this, or has determined that such is not the case.

This also occurs when the supervisor is too far removed from instruction, is too stupid to balance things out, is not a team man, or otherwise. An "otherwise" will include arbitrariness, disenchantment with job or department, empire-building, or perhaps just an exhibition of a need for retraining on the part of that supervisor.

The trainer must insist that the students not be retrained. By criticizing student street performance through line supervisors he can consistently make necessary training modifications. But he must insist that academy and street practices be consistent and parallel.

Line supervisors, to this end, should be solicited for both evaluation and suggestion. An occasional academy tour for the supervisor will help in the balancing of the two worlds of classroom and street.

As always, the trainer must be able to sell his program to the administration. So he has to be a salesman, and sometimes unfortunately something of a politician. We do not espouse politics in police work; quite the contrary! But we are also realists, and know that internal politics do exist in law enforcement, as in all businesses and professions.

At best we can say the trainer must be a salesman. Should this smack of internal politics, again, hopefully not, then we can only requote an old saying: "All things in moderation, including moderation."

In any event, the training officer needs to sell the program. The program consists of a tour of duty at the Police Academy for Sergeants. The tour, depending upon how well the trainer has sold the program to the Chief of Police, may consist of a visit to one class or for one day, for a short tour with the students, or, more hopefully, for the complete basic school length.

The sergeant is already a trained, veteran policeman. We know that. The students do not know that. The sergeant, on the other hand, sometimes overestimates his own worth and importance—many men do, not only sergeants of police.

Seriously, a complete tour of the academy by a sergeant, sitting in as a sort of graduate student, can be healthy for the sergeant, the recruits, and the department as a whole. The sergeant should never be embarrassed by quick or trick questions. He should be allowed to excell at his strong points—shooting, techniques of arrest, whatever. In this way, the recruits' esteem for this sergeant is built up. The sergeant, in his own eyes, is again a proven man. Other sergeants will need to excell also, for the newly turned-out policemen will compare them with the student-sergeant at the academy. This is in much the same vein as a Marine always compares other noncommissioned officers with his original drill instructor in boot camp. It may sound trite, but it is true.

Sergeants and officers thus graduated to the line and to street work are normally most reliable to test for the results of the academy instruction. These are some of the people from whom to obtain future critiques and comparisons when endeavouring to gauge reliability of instruction against the realities, practicalities, and vicissitudes of the line and street work.

These men are reliable for this purpose because they are recently accomplished students (even the sergeant), they are new and young enough to readily compare school with street, and if properly trained, are still identified sufficiently with the trainer and his program to communicate realistically.

The sergeant is key in this program, for he is best able of all to properly evaluate the training results as applied on the street. It is particularly helpful if policy allows for the program to include the sergeant to take and supervise a complete squad of officers in their uniform street work, what better test? An experienced sergeant accompanies recruits through their schooling, and then supervises the squad in the field.

Rapport and teamwork certainly should prevail in such a situation! And, not least, it allows for a truthful feedback to the trainer so that he can properly continue the viable instruction and can update and upgrade otherwise.

PART II

BASIC TRAINING

Chapter 4

CLASSROOM TRAINING FOR RECRUITS

W HEN AN OFFICER is hired, he usually comes to the department full of enthusiasm and eagerness to get at the job of catching criminals.

Before we let him undertake that job, we must teach him the basic rudiments of the job, and hopefully instill him with enough knowledge and skill to stay alive.

Most training programs begin in the classroom, which is something of a let-down for the recruit who imagines himself doing rather than learning.

Class training must be pertinent, timely and stimulating to be worthwhile. This is the responsibility of the training officer.

Each instructor must be adequately prepared for his class. He must know his subject and have an orderly method of presenting his lessons. It is not enough for him to be an outstanding officer with broad experience. Communication must be established and maintained if learning is to take place.

First consider the physical surroundings. Both student and instructor must be comfortable and adequately equipped. It is not necessary to have a room that will function only as a classroom, but the room selected should be functional for the purpose.

The student desks should be designed to accommodate either right or left handed students. They should be adequate to be comfortable for a large adult, and space provided for book storage. Be sure when placing desks in the classroom that ample space is provided between them to allow for good visibility and free movement.

The instructor must be equipped with a lectern, blackboard, and any other equipment he may require. Special equipment might be borrowed from a school or college for short periods, or rented when needed. This will greatly reduce your budget expenditures.

Communication must be established and maintained if learning is to take place.

The classroom must have good lighting, and be arranged in a manner that will allow darkening when films are to be shown. Heavy curtains or shades usually will be sufficient.

One very important thing to consider is the location of the classroom. A classroom located in a busy portion of the building, where there are likely to be many distractions or noises will severely hamper the instructor.

If possible select a room away from the general business spaces of your building. If one is available, an inside room without windows opening onto the street is best.

Having considered the plant and problems of the physical surroundings, we may now look to the problems of schedules, lesson planning, and curriculum.

Just as you would not expect a man to repair sophisticated electronic equipment without training, you must not expect a man to carry out the involved duties of a police officer without first providing him with the best possible background.

In this writing we have included a sample schedule for a recruit training program. You will note we have provided for early training concerning rules and regulations, and departmental procedures. Throughout the training we will be placing emphasis on the application of the rules and procedures, thus the man becomes familiar with them and forms his work habits accordingly.

"Okay, men, turn to page thirty-six."

While this chapter deals with classroom training, you will note the schedule calls for field exercises and physical training as well. We feel it is important to provide some relief from the tedium of lecture and notetaking. No matter how comfortable the furniture you have, sitting in one position for long periods is discomforting, especially for active young men.

We recommend early training in your method of report writing, and then application of the method in future course material. For example, if the lesson is robbery, have the student write a sample report showing the elements of the crime in a hypothetical situation, perhaps selected from a real crime reported in a newspaper.

We feel this method of training will serve to greatly reinforce the report writing ability of the men, and it serves as a constant test of the application of the material presented in lecture.

We have included in our schedule classes in spelling and basic English. We learned by sad experience that our system of public education often fails to provide these basic communication skills. We are sure any administrator can appreciate how easily writings can be misinterpreted if not properly structured. A crime report or record of arrest is no place for clarity to be lacking.

Certain areas of training in our sample schedule will obviously overlap. We feel this practice is good, to provide the emphasis needed to implant important facts or attitudes.

We recommend that the various classes on the schedule be taught by a number of instructors, people with experience in certain areas. We also recommend the introduction of guests to lecture in some areas. This relieves the training officer of some of his responsibilities, and provides the students with some variety in approach, as well as the benefit of a rich bank of experience.

We recommend that all instructors and students be given a clearly spelled out listing of class regulations and procedures and that the training officer supervise to see that they are adhered to.

By no means do we suggest a long list of rules and regulations. We do suggest basic rules concerning behavior in class, tardiness, and participation are necessary to a well-run program. It must be a basic responsibility of each instructor to support and enforce the rules.

We recommend that each officer be required to keep a notebook which is to be considered as a part of his grade in the program.

We suggest that rough notes from class be typed in outline form, and any appropriate handout material be placed in the notebook, preferably a three ring loose leaf binder.

The notes serve many purposes. The officer may use them for reference as he encounters situations in his work, or when preparing for promotion. The supervisor can easily see what the man was taught in class. This can be important when a question of procedure or department policy arises. If, for example, a disciplinary problem arises and there is a question whether the man knew the rule he has violated, or the procedure he has failed to follow, his notebook should reflect his training and help to answer the question. It will provide an area of proper defense for the man and show the need for training, or it will serve as evidence against him.

The notes will also provide a measure of how well the teacher is covering his subject matter.

As a practical suggestion we urge that your recruits be required to wear a training uniform. This may be something different from your usual duty uniform, perhaps the regulation uniform for the department, if no training uniform is provided for.

Wearing uniforms and being frequently inspected will create a solidarity of feeling among the men and inspections will serve to implant the proper air of discipline. It is important that during this period of training pride in appearance and conformity to regulations governing appearance be stressed.

This discipline should apply not only to the recruit but to the training officer as well. Whenever an instructor normally works in uniform, that is how he should appear when he lectures the men. We do not suggest that people who do not wear uniforms in their daily work should adopt them for classes.

Instructors should be familiar with the schedule for the recruits and work to keep as close to the timing as possible.

They should be prompt and businesslike in their classes and make every effort to support the overall aims of the training program.

A maverick instructor who deviates from policy, or who spends a large part of his time telling jokes or exciting stories may be a very popular fellow, but his lesson may suffer, as will class discipline.

For this reason the training officer should frequently monitor classes.

TRAINING BULLETIN # 136
SUBJECT: RECRUIT TRAINING SCHOOL
        AUGUST 1971
        10 WEEKS—INSTRUCTION AND PATROL
SOURCE: DALY CITY POLICE DEPARTMENT
PURPOSE: OUTLINE AND SCHEDULE OF COURSES
AUTHOR: TRAINING DIVISION
        STEEN #23 7-28-71

A. Introduction:

The following course outline and schedule is proposed by the Training Division with Approval of STAFF BUREAU and CHIEF.

With the idea that the four involved trainees have all had some Police experience and have all had either Departmental or other formal schooling in the Police Science curriculum, the present schedule of instruction and patrol is generally divided into an eight-hour day, half in the classroom and half on the street.

Also, since these are advanced Police Science students, the technical areas, as distinct from Departmental Policy and Procedure areas, are anticipated to be at this level of learning.

However, the course as outlined is not rigid. The instructor should be flexible enough to gear his instruction to actual learning levels and student needs. The only requirement is that well trained Officers, in basics and Policy, be turned out on the street.

Training is a continuing and on-going process. When class is out and the class notebook closed, training has not stopped. Examination and evaluation is also a continuous process.

It is expected that study habits and discipline will be developed, that study assignments will be made and carried out, that the Officer's field and class notebooks will be current and with class notes typed, organized, and examined at frequent intervals.

Supervisors and instructors should accumulate data, from observation and testing, sufficient to document their periodic Evaluation Reports. Patrol Supervisors are asked to formally evaluate the trainee weekly.

LESSON PLANS—In preparing for each of his instructional assignments, the Instructor must prepare a lesson plan in advance. This lesson plan should be tailored for alloted time, should include theory, the law, the SOP, Departmental Policy, should include personal experience, and should include citations and bibliography. Test questions should also be provided to Training Division, who will be testing at frequent intervals as soon after completion of instructional blocks is complete.

B. Instructors and Courses

Note: The rest of this material appears on Pages 219-221, under TRAINING DIVISION BULLETINS.

Chapter 5

FIELD TRAINING FOR RECRUITS

F IELD TRAINING EXERCISES during recruit training are important for a number of reasons. They provide a break from the tedium of the classroom and thereby help to keep the students enthused.

The field exercises also provide an opportunity for practical application of the things they are being taught in the classroom.

It is interesting to note that men who do not do well in the classroom often perform very well in the field. They are people who prefer doing rather than hearing about procedures.

Field exercises should be well planned to coordinate application of a number of things the student has learned in class.

For example, a murder scene might be staged. The students must sketch and photograph the scene, interview witnesses, take notes, mark evidence and all the other steps that go into such an investigation. Thus they are applying the many things they have been taught.

As a final touch the instructor could have the men submit complete crime reports on the incident, including an arrest.

If your time and facilities permit, the lesson could be expanded to include a mock trial in which the recruits would testify to their parts in the investigation. In such an effort a member of the district attorney's staff might serve as an advisor. If available, a friendly judge might permit use of his court and act as judge in the case.

There are a wide variety of training exercises that lend themselves very well to field programs. Firearms training, driver training, self-defense, searches and many others can be used.

We have included within this book a chapter dealing with the use of video-tape, and other aids.

Field exercises provide an excellent opportunity to put such tools to work. If each man can view himself going through his part of an exercise, he can see his own strong or weak points, and correct where necessary.

In the opinion of the authors field exercises are only valuable when properly staged. Equipment to perform the job, props, and personnel must be available.

"Don't be alarmed. This is a training exercise."

The location for such programs must be carefully selected. It is not good to place the officers in a position where they will be under the public eye and unduly embarrassed. Neither should you alarm citizens by creating the appearance of a serious crime or disaster.

Do not place obstacles in the way of your students by making the situation too complicated when you offer a field problem. At the same time, making the problem too simple removes the challenge and reduces the value of the exercise.

Be sure all students are equipped with the tools they need to carry out the task. Provide them with a list of materials some time prior to the class and make them responsible to assemble their equipment.

As a word of caution, make the watch commander aware of your presence and purpose if you are to be in public.

The authors recall with chagrin an exercise in surveillance conducted with members of an academy class. The officers were assigned to a "hound and hare" situation in a large shopping center, with teams of officers following "suspects." Unfortunately the police department in the city involved was not informed, and they were alerted to "suspicious" happenings by merchants in the center who observed the behavior of the officers and their quarry. Fortunately it all worked out.

During any field exercise the training officer or instructor should be present to evaluate the proficiency of the men and grade their performance. This will reveal any areas of training that might need to be reinforced in class.

Included herein is a sample plan for a field training exercise. You will note it clearly spells out the location, time, and purpose of the program as well as making assignments listing equipment and uniform.

As a practical matter a training uniform, possibly consisting of coveralls with department insignia, boots, and helmet, will make field training easier and certainly less wearing on expensive uniforms. We recommend use of such a uniform through recruit training, both in the class and in the field.

TO: Concerned Personnel

FROM: David A. Hansen
           Captain

SUBJECT: Riot Control Training
           0800-1700hrs 12-7-71

PLACE: Daly City Police Department   Locker Room
         90th/Sullivan Streets   Squad Room
         Daly City, Calif.   Police Parking Lot

PARTICIPANTS: (a) The 2nd Class, Peace Officers Standards and Training Basic School, College of San Mateo

(b) Trainer, Lecturer, Squad Leaders, and Video Recording Team (Daly City Police Personnel)

UNIFORM: (a) Helmet w/face shield

(b) Utility Uniform (open collar, police blue is optional)

(c) Bloused Boots

(d) Gas Masks

(e) Riot Stick

(f) Leather Gloves

(g) Gun Belt, Holster, and Revolver (the gun belt will be free from impedimenta such as keys, cuffs, and the like)

(h) Sweatshirt (optional, but recommended)

LOGISTICS: (a) Coffee and doughnuts will be available in the morning; the class will provide a clean-up detail.

(b) Soft drinks will be available for purchase during class breaks.

(c) Participants will lunch in the locker room. They will bring a bag lunch. Sandwiches can be sent in; to do this the class and details should send a collection to Training Division, DCPD ($1.00 per man) no later than two working days prior to the training.

EQUIPMENT: (a) Radios, handi-talkie (Squad Leaders)

(b) Gas Masks, extra

(c) Riot Sticks, extra

(d) 16mm projector

(e) Training Film

(f) Video Tape Camera, tape deck, and monitor

(g) Coffee Urn and cups

SCHEDULE:

0800-0830	Assembly, Roll Call, Issue of Necessary Equipment	LOCKER ROOM
0830-0920	Lecture, Chalk Talk	LOCKER ROOM
0930-1045	Stick Training	PARKING LOT
1055-1130	Training Film	SQUAD ROOM
1130-1200	Lunch	LOCKER ROOM
1200-1230	Video Tape Film	SQUAD ROOM
1230-1615	Riot Formation and Drill	PARKING LOT
1615-1700	Critique, and review of VTR tape of exercise	SQUAD ROOM

ATTENDANCE: Members of the POST class, CSM are required to attend, and will be evaluated and graded.

Any detail from outside agencies participate at the behest of that agency, as a joint exercise. Administrative control remains with that agency.

The Daly City Police Personnel are assigned to I Squad as their regular duty day.

David A. Hansen
Captain
Daly City Police Department

Chapter 6

POLICE ACADEMY AND
INTERDEPARTMENTAL TRAINING

IN LARGE CITIES and departments, academy training is usually an "in-house" program. In smaller jurisdictions much reliance must be placed on community academies serving a number of departments. Such programs are usually carried on under the auspicies of a community college.

The authors have found there are many advantages and disadvantages to such programs and will attempt to be objective in describing them.

Area academies allow officers to become acquainted with officers from neighboring departments.

It is good experience and broadening for officers to meet and become well aquainted with officers of neighboring departments. Such contacts will help to establish lines of communication between departments and can result in better performance.

The fact that instructors for such academy programs are usually drawn from agencies in the area gives the men an opportunity to see things through the eyes of experienced officers whose points of view often vary.

In many cases teaching groups of thirty to fifty men in a class can be productive. An academy can handle most of the recruit officers in a community and provide a high standard of training in the basics of law enforcement.

There are also some drawbacks which are encountered. An example of this is an area where there are political conflicts between cities or departments and such conflicts are allowed to be felt in the teachings of the instructors. Power-plays are frequent in such situations, and people are trying to force their influence on the administration of the program in order to have control over the direction of the program.

Administrators should have the support of the chiefs of the various departments involved, and be insulated against such political pressures as much as possible.

While it is an advantage to draw instructors from the various involved agencies, there is also the danger that such instructors will spend much of their time trying to convert recruits to their policies or procedures, rather than taking an academic approach to their subject matter.

It may be appropriate to describe the practice within the department, but it is not professional to attempt to "put-down" the practices of other departments. Such influence on the minds of inexperienced officers might result in creating an atmosphere of poor morale or lack of confidence in the department for which they work. If an experienced "teacher" puts forth negative opinions of the abilities and practices of their leaders they must feel there is some reason for the criticism.

A similar problem exists when various departments are mixed in an academy if there is a marked differential in pay scale, work-

A detailed notebook.

ing conditions, or fringe benefits between departments. Men may become disillusioned with their own department and the grass may look greener in other pastures.

Obviously, the mature, thinking, officer will be little influenced by such things. He is usually the man who makes plans well and is fully aware of the advantages and disadvantages of the various agencies before he takes his position. The immature, inexperienced man is the common victim of the insecurity described here.

There are many other problems that can crop up in community academy programs, such as whose facilities will be used, what controls shall be exercised over the men to maintain class discipline, and what uniforms will be worn or not worn.

Such problems may seem petty, but they can be real and difficult to solve.

We feel it is best to have the school on neutral ground. If such a location is to be the campus of the college sponsoring the program, the coordination of the program must be clearly spelled out and the chiefs must have ample control and influence in the direction of the program.

The isolated police academy.

The classroom must be large enough, and situated in a convenient location, preferably out of the mainstream of the campus.

It is distasteful that many students violently object to police officers being taught on campus, and more distasteful that some college administrators are sympathetic to their behavior.

We do not hold with the feeling that the officers should be hidden from sight. We do feel their classroom should be in an area where they will be undisturbed by the offensive conduct of the students as much as possible.

It will aid in the concentration of the students and reduce the possibilities of ugly incidents taking place, should militant students engage in provocation.

As with the suggestions rendered concerning recruit training within the department, we include the suggestion that in college-housed programs a guideline for discipline be set forth and the officers in attendance be completely, uniformly, briefed in what is expected of them should some problem arise on campus. No one can afford to have a police class become embroiled in a fight or riot situation. Regardless how right the policemen might be, they will suffer in the eyes of the public.

It is our strong recommendation that an officer of supervising rank be selected by the chiefs to act as disciplinary officer for an academy class.

It should be the responsibility of this man to keep attendance, conduct inspections and maintain the general class discipline during break periods. His authority must be clear and each man in the class must be required to respect his authority.

In the event that a serious problem arises the disciplinary officer must report the incident to the chief of the offender's agency and formal discipline carried out there.

To assist in maintaining discipline and for the general operation of the class, it is well to have officers in the class function as "squad leaders." If the contributing agencies have equal numbers of men in attendance then the senior of those men should be selected as squad leaders. If there are unequal numbers, a squad should be made up of five to eight men and a senior man placed in the squad leader post.

The squad leader will have the responsibility to collect work assignments, report absences for court or other reasons to the class leader, and serve as a pivot man when officers are lined up for inspections, or for training that requires such formation.

In many states there are requirements that officers attend specific training classes, such as the POST requirements in California.

In such situations the course is usually clearly delineated and the number of hours required for each topic spelled out. The examination procedure is also clear and results usually lead to a certificate and some college credits for the recruits.

It is usually the practice for the coordinator of the program to collect lesson plans, examination material, and any hand-out materials from the instructors. Such material should be maintained in a permanent file and available to any interested parties to review for content and suitability.

Colleges are subject to high turnover of personnel and coordinators come and go frequently. For that reason we submit that a master file of such material should be available to the chiefs. This negates the constant demand for material on the instructor and provides a control over the material.

Lesson plans and examinations should be up-dated whenever new or drastically changed procedures or decisions make such change necessary.

The authors recommend that each chief, or his designated aide should attend some classes during the program. It insures that the instructors are doing an adequate job and provides the men with first-hand knowledge that someone cares about their welfare.

At the completion of the program each recruit should be requested to submit an anonymous evaluation of the various instructors, with any comment he feels appropriate concerning individuals or the program at large. Such evaluation can be invaluable in deciding which instructors need training, or need to be replaced.

Finally, we recommend that each officer be required to keep a detailed notebook on all his classes, to be submitted as a part of his final grade in the program.

Each notebook should be checked periodically during the program to see the men are getting the information they need and the notebook should be emphasized as a valuable product of the class, which they may use again and again in the future.

There are many instances beyond recruit training that are handled well involving more than one department.

One situation that lends itself to this kind of training is riot control methods. Getting enough men together for such an exercise may not be possible for a small or medium-sized department. Combining the units of two or three departments might make such a venture much more practical.

There is dual value in such a situation. The men are trained, and they are trained in uniform methods. Such training could be vital if they are called together in a mutual aid situation.

There are many areas that are well-suited to both formal department-sponsored training or off-duty, seminar-type training.

We recently had the experience of attending classes with members of four other police departments on the subject of "Communications Models For Police." This was a program under the auspices of the University of California, for which the attending officers earned college credit.

The purpose of the program was to explore and better understand both internal and interdepartmental communications, and thereby improve our operations and relations with one another.

The value of the program was immeasurable. We got rid of many false impressions about other departments and we learned the importance of clarity and sincerity in both verbal and written communications.

As with all such programs we all left with the feeling of better understanding of one another and our common problems in law enforcement, and a feeling of solidarity in our purpose.

As in the case of the described communications class, there may be funds available under LEEP* or some similar source to cover the costs of the individual officers.

*Law Enforcement Education Program

If the meetings are held in the spaces of one of the police agencies and the officers combine to pay the costs of refreshments, there is no other expense to be met.

We have found that in the class setting where all of the officers are students and equals that many of the usually patrolman-supervisor barriers will fall and all can benefit from the experience.

At times some person or organization in a community may have something to offer that would benefit law agencies greatly. It speaks well of a department that invites others to participate in such a program.

Such an effort spreads the benefit to colleagues and greatly enhances the image of the department in the eyes of others.

A training program offered by the F.B.I., or some similar agency is often made available with the stipulation that a minimum number of people attend. Combining forces will often meet that requirement and the benefit of the program can be gained rather that missed.

We urge administrators to communicate with their neighbors and when common need for training exists, and the program can be fitted to such use, combined operations be undertaken.

PART III
CRITICAL AREAS OF TRAINING

Chapter 7

REPORT WRITING

THE METHOD of reporting that is available to the officer is not important to this writing. The fact that the officer makes one or numerous official police reports during each tour of duty is most important.

The officer may handwrite, or handprint, typewrite, or dictate his reports. He may dictate to a stenographer or to a machine, from which the typist will, then or later, extract and reduce to the printed word.

These are reporting methods. The subject matter to be discussed herein is that of "reporting." Because of its general acceptability and wide use, we will use here the term "report writing," to include a police report on paper, regardless of how that report came to be imprinted on that paper.

First, let us discuss and dismiss the form report. While housekeeping reports and logs, maintained on appropriate forms, are necessary, the police report on a form, the filling in of little boxes, is anathema to the authors.

A form report is a crutch. By the very questions in the boxes-to-be-filled-in, the reporting officer's thinking is slanted. The very choice of the form itself tends to slant the thinking of the officer, causing him to report subjectively rather objectively and with a clear mind.

Let us assume the death of a citizen. Which form report will the officer choose to execute? Does he utilize the Dead Body Report? The Homicide Report? The Suicide Report? The Fatal Auto Accident Report?

If several of the factors are present, which report form takes precedent over the others? Does the fact that the person died in an auto collision tend to make the officer investigate an "auto accident," necessarily, rather than to approach the matter as a possible homicide?

"So this is the new All-Purpose police form?"

We find that form reports often are the building blocks to an empire under construction. Policemen fill in little boxes so that someone, in their own or another agency, can extract statistics to use in their kingdom building.

Perhaps the statistics are necessary to the bureau or agency— but is it really productive to have an officer select from a myriad of forms, those omnipresent and ubiquitous forms, to fill in? How often does an officer, who really has better things to do, find himself required to fill in several different forms when reporting a single case? All too often, say we!

This is not, however, a treatise to end form reports. Rather it is an introduction to the importance of training officers in proper and meaningful communication via the police report. The police trainer will find few subjects more important than this is to impart to the policemen. The police officer will find few subjects more important for him to learn.

At the very least, the officer will study few subjects that he will perform more often than that of report writing. Oftentimes the officer will not be enamored of the subject of report writing. Often he will avoid it when and where possible, and often he will endeavor to avoid it when such avoidance is really not feasible.

An officer will sometimes practice at the pistol range once or more each month. Yet, even in these troubled times, that officer stands an excellent chance of never having to fire his weapon while on duty. Even should he be required to fire his revolver, the odds are long against his needing to do so often, far less than his having to shoot on each tour of duty.

He will, however, need to write at least one report nightly, and often many, many more than that. Thus, an officer who is weak on report writing, would behoove himself to practice that report writing. The trainer, therefore, needs to approach report writing training seriously and on a continuing basis.

The trainer must be himself schooled in English composition and in spelling. He should start training the new officer in spelling. Elsewhere in this book the reader will find a list of words that are commonly used in police work and which are as commonly misspelled.

As the police receive more and more new men with college backgrounds, we find that generally they are better schooled than were the teamster types of yesteryear. (This is not designed to defile or degrade former teamsters!) They are better schooled generally, that is, but they neither write sentences nor spell words as well as did/do the erstwhile teamsters. In some ways, one might make a good argument that students are not taught to read and write while in school in this present day!

Free thinking, and "I grade for thought not for neatness," or "I grade for content and not for spelling" may be all very well, but it is harmful to police work. An officer needs to spell properly or he may well be destroyed in the eyes of the jury while undergoing a blistering cross examination by the defense attorney.

Spelling is important, too, in terms of filing. A misspelled name is a misfiled name.

An investigator may pay attention to details. The spelling of a name can be construed to be a detail. The officer who consistently is sufficiently inattentive as to the proper spelling of the name of the witness or suspect, can be expected to overlook other details in the course of his investigation.

Adherence to good spelling procedures, in-service or recruit training in spelling, and the like, serve a twofold purpose: improved spelling results, and the mind is trained, at least to some extent, to pay attention to details.

Writing is a means of communication between the writer and the reader. The reader does not always understand the message. When this is so, then the writer has wasted the time of both the writer and the reader.

We should give more thought to the language we use. This language, this tool of communication, is used to think and to communicate. Since the words that make up the language can be misunderstood, it is axiomatic that we should take pains that it is not misunderstood. If it is important enough to communicate, it is important enough to understand, it is important enough to write selectively and adroitly, and it is important enough to think about first and to approach carefully.

A report is a written or verbal account of something. A police report is a record of police services performed.

Reports become permanent records. The records serve to preserve facts for prosecution, and to list property lost, stolen, or recovered. Through the records we are able to determine the activities, habits, and descriptions of individuals.

Reports can also help to protect falsely accused officers by establishing a code of conduct of the officer, his approach to matters as previously reported, as well as to the degree of competence exhibited in past investigations.

For the police supervisor, reports aid in determining whether a case was properly investigated. The quality of a police officer's work is reflected in his reports; this in turn assists in evaluating the individual officer, as well as pointing up training needs and/or defects.

Reports provide a record of offenses known to the police, as well as a record of offenses cleared. This enhances the statistical records.

The compilation of statistics aid in the eventual tactical deployment of the patrol force. This is accomplished through the tabulation of business volume in terms of what is happening by time of day and by geographical area. The police leader can then assign his strength to locations when and where the action is.

What are the requisites of a satisfactory report? The report must be complete as to all necessary details. It needs to be as brief as is consistent with the enscribing of all the essential features in a clear and understandable manner.

Accuracy is essential, and relates to those things which have actually happened and which have been verified through investigation. The officer's conclusions belong in a place in the report format which call for conclusions; conclusions must not be intermixed with the established facts of the matter at hand.

Legibility and the need for it go with good spelling; i.e., if the reader cannot read and understand it the writer has wasted the time of both the writer and the reader.

Good grammar is as important as good spelling. Again, we do not want to provide the defense attorney with an opportunity or ammunition with which to cross-examine the officer on the witness stand with the goal of making him into an apparent dunce before the jury.

When and where abbreviations are utilized, the reporting officer must be imbued with the habit of abbreviating correctly. Policemen seem to develop the habit of over abbreviation, using incorrect abbreviations, and in fact manufacturing abbreviations.

Reports are essentially answers to stock questions. The questions to be answered are known as the "Five W's." The five W's to be answered are **WHO, WHAT, WHEN, WHERE, WHY,** and **HOW.** The Trainer needs to instill into his charges the ability to automatically answer these questions in each report. The formula is as important to the reporting officer as is the five paragraph combat order to the military leader.

"**WHO?**" means all persons concerned with the case. "**WHO?**" includes the suspect (s), victim, witnesses, reporting party, investigating officer, attending doctor, everyone connected with the matter at hand. "**WHO?**" includes name, age, color, residence, business address, telephone number and any and all other identifying data.

"**WHAT?**" demands an answer to what took place. What has happened to cause the report to be made in the first place? The amount of detail, of course, depends upon the nature and purpose of the report.

"**WHEN?**" asks when did the incident occur? When was it discovered? When was it brought to the attention of the police? This is essentially the fixing of time, and there is more than one time involved in every report. "Time" in this instance includes day, date, time, month and year.

"**WHERE?**" asks the location of occurrence. Also to be included is the location of the object to which the reporter wishes to call the attention of the reader. The reporter will want to give address, floor, apartment number, part of the room involved, direction of the street, and perhaps the nearest intersection. Not only does the officer describe his evidence or property, but most important, and often neglected, is **WHERE IS THE EVIDENCE NOW?**

"WHY?" is answered, in the case of a crime, in terms of motive. Why did the incident occur? Was it murder for revenge, assault as a result of a drinking bout, an auto accident as a result of an engineering defect, or excess speed, or whatever?

"HOW?" means simply, in the case of a crime, modus operandi. What was the method of operation? How did the incident occur?

The foregoing are the ingredients essential to every police report. They are introduced against the backdrop of a writing style. This style of writing is known as the "4 S FORMULA." The "4 S FORMULA." is **SHORTNESS, SIMPLICITY, STRENGTH, AND SINCERITY.**

SHORTNESS requires that the reporter not repeat what was said in another report. Needless words and phrases should be avoided, as should roundabout phrases such as, "in reference to" and "with regard to." Except when making a direct quote, which should of course be painfully accurate, the reporter does better to say "graft" than to say "eleemosynary," for example.

SIMPLICITY involves the reporter in knowing what he is going to write. Again, it involves the use of short words, sentences, and paragraphs. The writer needs to tie his thoughts together so that the reader can follow them from one to the other without getting lost.

STRENGTH means for the writer to use specific concrete words. The more active verbs should always be used. "The woman shot him," for example, is better, stronger, than "he was shot by the woman." Answers are to be given first, and followed by any necessary explanation. To explain an answer before giving it is to confuse and lose the reader. To say "it appeared to be blood" is weak. Say it was blood. If an explanation is necessary, then the reporter might say "the man was bleeding, the substance looked like blood, and it tested out to be blood."

SINCERITY means for the reporter to be human. Policemen are forever being modest, jargonistic, officialese. To be human means to make the report more readable by using human terms. "I, you, he, she, we" are better for this purpose, and shorter, than the jargonistic and unreal, stiff, "reporting officer, this officer, these officers, the undersigned."

Mistakes should be admitted, and negative information included in any police report.

The trainer needs to be adamant and merciless in his attack on the use of jargon. He will have to insist that his recruits learn to write simply and to avoid the use of officialese.

Later, in in-service training and refresher classes, he will have to re-do the job, for policemen invariably backslide in this area.

The trainer, then needs to also work on the police supervisor to this end. If jargonistic reports are habitually approved by the sergeant, for example, jargon will again become habit to the reporting officers.

This is an extremely difficult cross which the trainer must bear. He should be continually on the attack against the use of jargon. Policemen tend to become legalistic in thinking and language. Their very life style, officially speaking, tends to put policemen in this bag.

Policemen also tend to speak in numbers. They are ineluctably inundated with code language. They work in a climate of Penal code, Vehicle Code, Radio Code, and the like. The codes become their language, and the language filters into police reports.

The report exists for the reader and for no other purpose. The report does not exist for the writer; it exists for the reader. Thus, should the reader be unable to understand the report, then the writer has wasted the time of himself and the reader. A jargoned-out report may very well obscure an otherwise excellent investigative effort.

Given the use of the **Five Ws** and the **4 Ss**, then we only need write the report in the English language for it to be understood. To write in officialese and/or code numbers, he may as well compose his message in Hindustani or Swahili, for the reader will not understand it.

Again, this is a difficult tendency for the trainer to overcome. The policemen actually speak in this foreign language. How often have we heard a conversation something like this? "After the 459 I proceeded north on Mission and on-viewed a 415 involving several 647Fs. I called for cover. Jones arrived Code 3. One of the guys was a 148. He and Jones were treated at County, and all the bodies were booked. I damned near missed Code 7 at 10-10."

What the officer is saying, translated to English, is this: "After investigating the burglary, I drove north on Mission Street, and saw a fight involving several drunks. I asked for assistance, and Jones came hurriedly. One man resisted arrest. He and Officer Jones were treated at County Hospital. All persons were arrested. I was quite late getting home for my assigned meal hour."

Too, when reports go to other states, or to the F.B.I., the code number "459" or "211" are peculiar to the California Penal Code. What the other agency, the reader, is interested in, is not "459" or "211," but in the fact that we are endeavoring to relate facts about a burglary or a robbery.

DALY CITY POLICE DEPARTMENT
REPORTS—THE CATEGORY METHOD

I. All police reports will be composed by the Category method.

    A. This method will be utilized regardless of the means of making the report.

        1. The Category method will be employed upon the Offense Report.

        2. The Category method will be employed upon all form reports with the exception of the Property Report, which is always supplemental to other reports.

            a. When a form report is used, and information normally belonging in a Category has already been included within the form provided, the reporting officer will include the Category, followed by the words "See Above."

3. Numerical radio code designations and other than standard acceptable abbreviations will not be utilized within any category.

II. The Category method of reporting will consist of nine categories, with Category four subdivided into two parts. Each individual Category, or portion thereof, is limited by definition, but not by length. A Category may be any necessary length; the fact that a police report should be as concise as possible should be a guiding factor here. A Category may consist of one sentence, or one or more paragraphs. The designation "N/A" will be used where the Category is inapplicable.

A. The first Category will be designated as follows:
"1—SUMMARY" (Synopsis)

1. The summary will be a concise and accurate story of the entire incident to date including the dates and times during which the incident occurred.
2. The summary will not include the date and time of the investigation nor the initial reporting time.
3. The summary will include the modus operandi, where applicable.

B. The second Category will be designated as follows:
"2—VICTIMS AND WITNESSES"

1. These will be listed by name, and will include:
   a. Address
   b. Race
   c. Sex
   d. Age
   e. Residence address and telephone number
   f. Business address and telephone number
2. In Accident Reports, it is only necessary to designate the vehicle in control of the respective driver, following the driver's name, in lieu of other identifying data.
3. Victims, where there are more than one, will be designated V #1, V #2, V #3.

a. Victims should be given this designation in Category 2.

b. Victims, when subsequently mentioned, will be refered to by this designation followed by the subject's surname.

c. If the same surname applies to more than one party in a reporting incident, each will be referred to by this designation, followed by the surname and the first initial of the given or Christian name.

4. Witnesses, where there are more than one, will be designated W #1, W #2, W #3.

a. Witnesses should be given this designation in Category 2.

b. Witnesses, when subsequently mentioned, will be referred to by this designation followed by the subject's surname.

c. If the same surname applies to more than one party in a reporting incident, each will be referred to by this designation, followed by the surname and first initial of the given or Christian name.

d. Witnesses shall include all persons interviewed regarding a given incident, including those with negative information, as well as every officer participating in the investigation.

C. The third Category will be designated as follows: "3—SUSPECTS"

1. When there is a suspect whose name is unknown, the word "Unknown" should be used in place of the suspect's name.

a. Should the suspect later become known, the word "Unknown" should be replaced by the suspect's name and identifying data.

2. When the suspect has been arrested, it is only necessary to record the name and arrest number in this category.

3. When the suspect has not been arrested, he should be described according to the following listed criteria:
   a. Name
   b. Address
   c. Race
   d. Sex
   e. Age
   f. Height
   g. Weight
   h. Build
   i. Color, type and style of dress of hair
   j. Color of eyes. State if glasses were worn and describe, if applicable.
   k. Complexion
   l. Identifiable physical defects, if any
   m. Clothing, including color, style and state of maintenance.

4. Suspects, where there are more than one, will be designated S #1, S #2, S #3.
   a. Suspects should be given this designation in Category 3.
   b. Suspects, when subsequently mentioned, will be referred to by this designation, followed by the subject's surname
   c. If the same surname applies to more than one party in a reporting incident, each will be referred to by this designation, followed by the surname and the first initial of the given or Christian name.

5. Suspects should be considered, although not limited to, all persons arrested, cited or upon whom a complaint charging a law violation is being sought.
   a. This will also apply to accident investigation reports.

D. The fourth Category will be divided into two parts. The first portion of that Category will be designated as follows:

"4–INVESTIGATION"

1. This Category should be reported in chronological diary form, from the point of view of the first person. Do not repeat the summary.

2. The investigation will commence with the date, day and time of the investigation.

3. The Category should include four areas.

   a. Investigative methods used.

   b. Facts established.

   c. Summarized statements expressed in general terms, if pertinent to the investigation.

   d. Negative as well as positive information.

      1. Example: If a witness has "seen and heard nothing," the information should be so recorded.

      2. This is designed to eliminate potential surprise defense witnesses.

E. The latter portion of the fourth Category will be designated as follows:

   "4a–CONCLUSIONS"

1. All factually substantiated conclusions should be contained therein.

2. Opinions reasonably deducted through investigative processes should be contained therein.

F. The fifth Category will be designated as follows:

   "5–PHYSICAL CONDITION"

1. When pertinent to the case, the condition of victims, witnesses and/or suspects should be noted. Physical Condition will refer to the physical, mental, emotional and state of sobriety of those persons.

   a. Condition before and after incident, if known, should be recorded.

   b. Officer will state what aid was rendered.

   c. Officer will state who rendered said aid.

2. If victim is hospitalized, officer should so state.
   a. Record name of hospital.
   b. Record who transported victim there.
   c. Record name of attending physician.

3. In cases wherein the sobriety of a suspect is a necessary portion of the Corpus Delecti, the listing of his condition in this category does not supplant the officer's responsibility to list all elements of the crime in Category 4.

G. The sixth Category will be designated as follows: "6—VEHICLES"

1. All vehicles pertinent to the case in any manner whatever are to be listed.
   a. Vehicles, where there are more than one, will be designated Veh. #1, Veh. #2, Veh. #3.

2. The following conventional descriptive manner will be utilized (CYMBaL) :
   a. Color
   b. Year
   c. Make
   d. Body, and
   e. License (State, or other jurisdiction, and number)

3. The vehicle should be further described as to damage.

4. The vehicle should be further described as to loud mufflers, and/or all other apparent mechanical abnormalities.

5. The vehicle should further be described as to stickers, decals and/or painted words or pictures.

6. If the vehicle is impounded, the reporting officer will state where, and by whom authorized.

H. The seventh Category will be designated as follows: "7—EVIDENCE"

1. The reporting officer will describe and itemize all physical evidence of the appropriate Property Report.

He will refer this Category to the appended **Property** Report Form.

2. He will state the exact location where said evidence was found.

3. He will state who found each item of evidence.

4. He will state where the evidence is located at the time of the report.

5. In cases where statements are obtained, refer this category to said statement, noting location where statement may be found, i.e.: Appended; Det. Div. file.

I. The eighth Category will be designated as follows.
"8—PROPERTY"

1. Itemize and completely describe each article taken on the appropriate Property Report Form. Refer this category to the appended Property Report.

2. Note where the property is located at the time of the report.

3. Record the value of each article taken.

4. List each available serial number.

5. Record any other identifiable markings.

J. The ninth Category will be designated as follows:
"9—CONFIDENTIAL OPINIONS"

1. When the reporting officer does not desire to utilize this Category, he will include the number heading on his report, and will follow this with the "N/A" symbol.

2. When the reporting officer does desire to utilize this Category, he will bring his complete report to completion, and will then indicate that a new page will be started for this Category.

3. Category 9 will always be separate from the main body of the report. This Category will never be given out to parties outside of this department for any reason whatever. This Category is designed to be a receptacle for

the officer's impressions of the case which he is unable to substantiate factually. It is here that he will record his suggestions and other remarks. These remarks may help to shape the direction of follow-up investigations. In fairness to the officer, he should not have to be accountable for them. Therefore, they will stay in this privileged class.

III. The Follow-up report in the category system.

A. Nothing in the Category system of report writing should be construed to mean a change in the present records system. The report system as such remains the same. The Category system is a method of putting words on paper to result in a police report. As a result, the follow-up report status is not changed by the Category system.

1. When reporting a follow-up investigation, the officer will list in Category #1 a brief synopsis of his initial summary, and, in addition, include the following:

a. The victim's designation followed by his surname.

b. A summary of recent events developed through investigation or information since the initial report.

2. In Category #2, the first designated victim and witness will be listed, followed by the respective surname applicable.

a. Should there be more than one victim or witness, the appropriate designation followed by the symbol "N/C" (no change) will be listed.

1. EXAMPLE: V #1—Jones
V #2 through V #5—N/C
W #1—Smith
W #2—N/C

3. In Category #3, the first suspect will be listed by designation, followed by his surname.

a. Should there be more than one suspect, the appropriate designation, followed by the symbol "N/C" will be listed.

b. If a previous listed witness later become a suspect, the following procedure will be followed:

1. Following the witness designation, the officer will record: "W #1 (or W #5, as the case might be) is now known as S #4 (or S #20, as the case might be)."

2. Henceforth, that witness designation will be carried, followed by the symbol "N/C."

3. The suspect is then listed in Category #3 and given the next available designation.

4. All other Categories (i.e. those wherein no change is necessary to be recorded) will be listed as "N/A" (not applicable or "N/C" (no change) as the case may be.

IV. The individual categories will always be listed with some information.

A. A Category will always contain either positive or negative information.

B. If a form report, where information will have been already related with respect to a particular category, said category will be listed by number and title, followed by the information "See Above."

C. If a Category is not pertinent to a particular case, this will be so stated.

1. The Category will be listed by number, but not by title, followed by the symbol "N/A," which is taken to mean "not applicable."

2. Should successive categories happen to be inapplicable to a given case, said categories may be combined for the purpose of listing the "N/A" symbol.

a. EXAMPLE: "5 thru 8 N/A"

b. The symbol "N/A" should not be confused with the word "Unknown" (see "D" next).

D. Whenever a Category is pertinent, but the information cannot or has not been established at the time the report is made, the Category should be numbered and titled, followed by the word "unknown." Reporting officer, or investigating officer, where these two are not the same man, should endeavor to add positive information in place of the word "unknown" in his follow-up reports.

V. The reporting officer, the person reading the reports, and the report.

A. The Category method is established so as to list information necessary to police reports in an orderly manner.

B. The Categories are arranged so as to be in an orderly, categorical, logical sequential order for the reporting officer.

C. Said Categories will logically fit any police report. They will be so used in this department.

D. Categories are limited by definition, but not by length, and are numbered so as to separate them one from the other.

E. Categories are titled so that they are readable and readily understandable by any authorized person outside of this department who may find occasion to read any report from the Daly City Police Department. Police investigations are recorded in instruments known as "Reports." The investigation, and the resulting report is never any good, anywhere, at any time, to anyone, if the information is not readily understood by the authorized reader. These are the reasons for the establishment of the Category report method, which has been incorporated within the Records System of this Department.

Chapter 8

GUN POLICY
THE MORAL AND LEGAL ASPECTS

T HE TRAINING officer will teach no more important subject ever than the departmental gun policy. In some ways, the trainer will experience no more difficult subject upon which it is necessary to instruct.

Too often too many departments have not had clear-cut gun policies. They may have taught the officers as to the use of the service revolver, but they instructed, if at all, very sketchily as to the policy concerning the use and the employment of that weapon.

A department may have listed among its rules some comments about guns. Usually these include some observations as to the need to report the discharge of a firearm for any reason. They also often include the necessity and need for shooting injured and dangerous animals when other means are not readily and safely available to the officer on the street. And, too, the autocratic disciplinarian traditionalists who wrote the rulebook have sought to protect and project the military structure of the department; they would have the officer shoot "in obedience to the order of a superior officer."

Some instruction from the penal code, or similar tome, will tell the officer of the legalistics. Unfortunately, after the fact newspaper stories instruct further on the realities of street shootings by policemen. We learn that the officer might have been legally and technically correct in a given case involving shooting, but that he was grossly in error in terms of mores, neighborhood expectations, and the like. A technically "correct" shooting, far from solving a bad situation, may escalate the problem into a full scale riot or insurrection.

The departmental administration often lives in a fool's paradise vis a vis policy matters. It is easy for the Chief to feel that he has a clear-cut gun policy, for example. The policy is certainly

"I don't know about you, but I don't feel comfortable."

clear to him. Whether or not there is an actual policy extant, it is not unusual for the troops not to know of it.

Now, to say that the troops actually do not know of the existence of a policy is to come on a little strong. The authors reiterate: too often the troops are unaware of a policy which the Chief feels does exist and is clear.

Another piece of the same problem: the official policy has been unofficially modified so often as to no longer resemble the Chief's thinking. The Chief sits in his office fat, dumb, and happy in the knowledge that he has a good policy. The troops have been told "how it really is" from street supervisors who have made the too-often exception or addition to the policy. These same supervisors would piously assure the Chief that all policy matters are being carried out. Yes, sir, they are really on top of the problem.

Then, too, because of problems resulting from police shootings in recent years, departments come out with sweeping proscriptions concerning the use of the gun. While the officer needs to know when NOT to use his weapon, there should be a positive statement somewhere that tells him when he can shoot. He is really entitled to know.

The training officer will need to determine just what is the departmental gun policy. Should it appear to him to be a clearcut policy, then he only needs to verify it.

He should gain an audience with the Chief, his staff officers and the planning and research people, where these latter are not the same as the former. The training officer needs to make several things clear, and must obtain clearcut decisions prior to his undertaking any form of gun policy instruction to the troops. The troops are confused enough without experiencing policy changes or "explanations" ex post facto to the next police shooting.

The training officer must have done his homework prior to the meeting. Too, the other participants should know what the meeting is going to be about; for it is not conducive to the establishment of rapport to surprise anyone or to catch them off guard. We suggest the trainer be prepared with "handouts," to include samples of all rules, regulations and directions concerning departmental gun policy extant.

As the meeting begins, the trainer should trace the gun policy history to the group. Then, issuing handouts, he might proceed as follows:

Gentlemen, in this first series of handouts, you will note, are covered our penal code sections, our rules and regulations, and our standard operating procedure relative to the gun policy, or more simply, when does the policeman shoot or not shoot.

This second group of handouts covers directives and memoranda issued by this department to the officers and to the news media. They include commendations to officers who have been involved in shootings, as well as reprimands and cautions to officers for warning shots and the display of the gun generally.

This third group of handouts includes copies of news stories where every lay expert in the world has commented following police shootings. These show the type of heat that may be expected to result from such occasions.

I am asking you to put these things together and to determine whether we have a viable gun policy, one that we will stick with when the chips are down.

This last handout shows what is recommended by the International Association of Chiefs of Police and what is recommended by other agencies. If we are sure we have a policy, and when we agree as to what the policy is, I can teach it (or reiterate it) to the men, without wasting their time and mine and with a minimum of confusion.

Should the department not have a gun policy, the meeting might be conducted as above, with the aim of making policy. It may be simpler to "make" policy at the meeting, using the methods delineated, than to rehash and remake old policy. The administration will not then have to unlearn anything before they can learn something new, not having learned anything in any event relative to this particular problem.

Should the trainer be unable to get a policy forged or endorsed (a distinct possibility, depending upon current staff suspicions and machinations), then the trainer can instruct only by example. He can utilize the same handouts he has shown to the Chief and his staff. He can trace the history of the use of the gun and of gun policy (obviously "in general" with the gun policy). He can and should illustrate for the officers what incidents have brought forth reward or reprimand from the department, what the laws and regulations say, what recent news commentary has been, and when policemen have been charged or suspended.

The trainer, if he does this carefully, should be able to project the trends and rather completely inform those whom he is charged with training.

On the other hand, in the more happy circumstance of having a forged and endorsed gun policy with which to work, he should ascertain that the Chief has put his name to the document. He is less likely to have to change horses in midstream in this fashion.

The actual teaching of the gun policy, mechanically or tutorially speaking, is found elsewhere in this book. Suffice here to state that the lecture method is largely applicable to recruit training, and the announcement or discussion method for in-service training. Recruits will accept the policy in good grace that will be in direct ratio to the trainer's molding of their professional and self-image.

The in-service officers are apt to receive gun policy training with cynicism. Some of this will be contrived, for the sake of "face," and some of it will be real. The policeman is a cynical man in a cynical business in a cold and cynical world. He will suspect gun policy to exist to restrict him, which in a sense it does. It is also there to protect him, and the trainer should make great effort to convince him of this.

And, within the limits of the policy, the trainer should also tell his officers **WHEN** to use the weapon (a good trainer will already have shown them **HOW** to use the gun). The officer is appropriately subjected to plenty of **DONT'S** in this matter; and he must also be shown the **DO**, or the **WHEN.**

The trainer must do his homework. There will be questions. It is probably best to have the Chief give announcement to the men via video tape recording, or in person where this applies, and then to have the trainer answer questions and give example as necessary.

Too often right-wing thinking officers will complain that their "hands are tied," that they are "second class citizens," and that the "brass doesn't care about us; in fact they don't know what is happening on the street."

Planned but candid answering on the part of the trainer, laced with humor and practicality, should be designed to show the officers both the realities of the problem and the care that trainers and supervisors should have for their officers.

Other officers will attack from another stance. Example: use the "shoot at the order of a superior officer," and some young modern will trot out and dust off the Nuremberg rule. This, too

When.

should be answered with care—no officer should try to obey an illegal order; yet "illegal" and "aggressive" may be divided by a fine line. The emergency situation is a poor place to discuss philosophies. The trainer should be certain to have a followup discussion with this man, perhaps when they next work on defensive tactics on the mats in the gymnasium.

It is important that the trainer document all segments of training given. It is extremely important that the trainer document the gun policy. He should be able to show when, where, to whom, and by whom the training was given on gun policy. The follow-up training needs also to be listed. Each man must be asked: Do you understand? An affirmative answer becomes a part of the documentation; a negative answer, of course, indicates the need for more training.

Where do the documentations go? They go into the trainer's files, to be sure. In case of a bad judgment call by a shooting officer, the department as well as the officer is on trial. The department needs to show proper instruction and training.

The Chief receives a copy of the documentation also. He should be able to show training statistics upon need.

Copies ideally should go to individual record jackets. It is unfortunate and necessary to start the ultimate personnel case through documentation of the initial training. That "first piece of paper" is all-important. The trainer is not usually the man who kicks off a personnel prosecution, but his by-product documentation shows both the trainer's worth and the necessary protection for the department when the officer goes significantly wrong.

Should the records not be filed owing to administrative policy, ineptness or caprice, the trainer's copies will suffice if and when, and hopefully not, the matter becomes an issue in the future.

SAMPLE GUN POLICY

It is the policy of this department to carry and use equipment as stated in the rules. Exceptions, if any, must be authorized in writing by the Chief of Police, without exception.

Platoon supervisors are charged through nightly inspections to periodically report compliance with this policy.

Weapons are to be drawn and exhibited when there is a reasonable apprehension that someone's life is in danger, be it that of a citizen or the officer.

The weapon may not be fired. That is, the suspect may surrender, or it may be shown that the danger subsided.

The officer who draws his weapon is prepared to fire it. He does not fire it for warning shots, or at buildings or autos or other inanimate objects. The weapon, when it must be fired, is to be fired at people. Fire to kill. There is no middle ground. If it is not important enough to kill, don't shoot.

Chapter 9

MECHANICS OF ARREST, SEARCH AND SEIZURE

IN APPROACHING the subject of arrest, the training officer must constantly emphasize the danger that may be involved in the most routine arrest. He must also thoroughly train his charges how to deal with that danger and stay alive.

It is a common fault of police officers that they let down their guard when dealing with drunks and traffic arrests. They take the approach that the offense is so minor that the person would not gain from trying to escape and therefore will not be violent.

No one knows how many police funerals resulted from such thinking. One is too large a number to excuse.

We make it a point to hire strong, alert, young men. We train them to think quickly and react to emergencies. Now we must impress on them the importance of never letting down.

It is a good practice to stage a demonstration early in this phase of training to emphasize the ease with which an opponent may disarm, and kill, an unwary officer. This is also a good time to have the students practice methods of approach, search, and handcuffing.

The search class is very effective if you provide a "suspect" who is carrying a large number of well concealed weapons. Allow students to conduct the search. Let the suspect demonstrate how he might overpower them if they err in procedure. When the search is over, have the "suspect" reveal anything the students missed. It is amazing to note that students often miss a gun in the crotch, hacksaw blades in the necktie, or similar large items.

We want that lesson learned in the classroom, where the most serious consequence is the ire of the instructor, and embarrassment before the class.

To be completely effective, this exercise should include such

74

We want the lesson learned in the classroom.

things as approaching the suspect, placing him in the least dangerous position and ending with handcuffing and a demonstration of methods of transportation.

Where possible, the demonstration should include methods employed with more than one suspect, and both one and two man police units.

As a preliminary to the actual exercise, there should be lectures and perhaps one of the recent films of the subject shown.

Another very effective aid might be photographs of an actual case of the murder of an officer. There is nothing like reality to drive home the point.

The object of the lessons is not to make the officer so fearful of people that he will not make a search or an arrest, but rather to instill in his mind the importance of alertness, caution and common sense. We all want to live to enjoy retirement. One mistake can end that dream.

"What prisoner?"

Once we have progressed through the arrest segment of this lesson, we must include the mechanics of handling the prisoner at the jail. It is pointless to bring him in from the street just to allow him to escape at the jail.

Every officer in your department should be able to function as a booking officer, and every officer must have thorough knowledge of the jail and its weak points.

As a trainer you must drum into their heads the importance of following proper procedure. Simple mistakes in the jail, or over-confidence in the search made on the street, has cost lives.

In an earlier writing (*The Police Leader—A Handbook,* Charles C Thomas, Publisher) we included a chapter on inspections. Within the chapter we comment on the importance of inspecting the police facilities. Nowhere is that inspection procedure more important than in the jail. We urge you to emphasize that procedure as a part of the procedure of each booking.

We feel it important to point out that very often it is not the recruit who makes the mistake that costs lives, but the older, experienced, officer, who has become too lax in his approach to the job.

Watch your officers as they process prisoners, or transport them to court. We are sure you will find the mistakes. Take an aggressive stand on this subject. Try to retrain as many of your men as you can, pointing out the mistakes you have observed.

By no means do we suggest humiliating anyone by name. The men will know when you are talking about them and they should learn from the mistakes.

In many departments the arresting officer is also required to "book" his prisoners and carry out identification procedures.

It is wrong to assume that everyone knows how to roll finger-prints or how to operate an identification camera. You must demonstrate and allow the men to practice if they are to accomplish the job properly.

It is also important the men learn the mechanics of the assignment of identification and/or arrest numbers, and the procedures for receiving and safekeeping the property of the prisoners.

Throughout you should continue to review and re-emphasize the lessons of safety, the importance of follow-up searches, and conformity to department procedure.

In our selection of lesson plans we included in this book is one of the subject of the mechanics of arrest.

THE OCCUPATIONAL HAZARDS OF LAW ENFORCEMENT.

As important as the mechanics of arrest and search, are the legal aspects involved.

An officer must know his limitations, and be fully cognizant of changes in law as they effect his ability to search, seize, and arrest.

Most states have set forth laws governing the circumstances under which an arrest may be made and the manner in which it should be done. Every officer must commit to memory those laws, and be guided by them.

Our Constitution wisely provided protections against unreasonable searches and seizures as a basic protection of freedom. We agree with that principle. Like most law enforcement people we also ascribe to the thinking that criminals must not be allowed to hide behind the shield designed to protect the innocent.

We have experienced many court decisions that have seemed to provide such protection. For this reason it is extremely important that we train our people how to use every legal means at their disposal in this war against the criminal.

We also feel it is important to accentuate the importance of employing the legally accepted means to the end. The arrest is our beachhead, the conviction the battle won.

Just as the founders of our country intended, we must also follow legal ground rules and protect the rights of the innocent citizen.

Many departments employ standard forms and procedures for use in obtaining search warrants, or in seizing property. Many others have handbooks prepared by the District Attorney or Attorney General which set forth the laws governing reasonable search.

If your department has no such handbook, we recommend that you obtain legal advice in preparing lessons in this area. We feel confident that most prosecuting attorneys would be only too happy to assist you. Certainly it makes their work easier if the police are following proper guidelines.

In this area of arrest and search, defense counsel constantly attack, searching for error or lack of understanding on the part of the officers. Save the men and the department from embarrassment by seeing that they are thoroughly trained and kept advised of significant changes in the law.

Inevitably the questions will come, "How much training have you had?" "Do you know the laws of arrest and when you can search?"

Give your men the ammunition they need to counteract this approach.

Having established the legal aspects of searches, your men must become skilled at the mechanical task of searching.

In the case of a person it is easy to teach a routine of search bringing into play overlaps and patterns of search.

In the case of buildings or areas of real estate it may be more difficult to work by preset patterns. You must teach a variety of methods, such as grid searches, spiral patterns or cross pattern searches. Armed with these methods in their arsenal of knowledge the officers can work efficiently with the best results.

This is the time to teach your officers the importance of being thorough in a search. It is also a good time to apply the methods of marking, collecting, and preserving evidence.

At all times, keep your men alert to the relationship of each job to the previous one and the one to follow.

An arrest may be lost because of the search. A conviction may be assured because proper legal processes were employed.

The sum total of the work performed must reflect in the police report if the prosecutor is to know what was done, who did it, and how sound is the case against the suspect.

Chapter 10

COMMUNITY AND PUBLIC RELATIONS

THE SUBJECTS OF COMMUNITY and public relations can be tied together for purposes of this chapter.

Generally we look upon community relations as being involved with minority groups in the community, or perhaps with special interest groups.

Public relations is viewed much in the light of Madison Avenue and the attractive package kind of approach to dealing with the public.

We submit that community and public relations are one and the same thing.

No department should be in such a position that it is slanting all its efforts toward one specific minority of citizens. As is implied in the title, community relations should deal with the relationship to the entire community.

We grant there are stresses in the relationship of police with many people of minority races. By no means do we wish to suggest turning our backs on the problems. We do say we cannot put all our efforts in one place and ignore the majority of the community who are entitled to equal benefit of our attention and services.

In approaching the subject matter the instructor must charge his students with responsibility to explore their own prejudices. It is a primary step in teaching the subject. If a man can eliminate at least the outward signs of his bias, he can then meet the public and attempt to give a proper image of the department.

Among the basic goals of any public or community relations program is implanting in the minds of the citizens the feeling the department cares about their welfare.

Such basic things as quick response to calls, or sympathetic comments when they are victimized, can support this impression.

An officer should be urged to show compassion and concern

81

for the problems of others. He should also be directed to perform his duty with as prompt and efficient a performance as he is able to render.

The officer should be instructed that his appearance and demeanor can either help or hinder him immensely. A man who looks clean, neat, and alert gives the impression of competence. If you alter that picture with a cruel, or cynical, expression on the face, in the mind of the citizen he becomes "cocky" or "hard."

There are times in law enforcement work to be hard and there may be a time when it is necessary to kill or be killed. There are also times to smile and offer warmth and comfort to people.

No officer should ever be allowed to forget that he too is a man, with faults and weaknesses, strengths and virtues, just as any other.

We have often heard officers complain about the attitude of the public. Administrators and supervisors have often had the opportunity to hear the citizens complain about the attitude and performance of the police. Somewhere between the two there is an area where both can give a little and relations can improve.

Since the police are organized and committed to public service, it falls with us to give first, to make that first move toward such improvement.

Police have long had the reputation as moochers or promoters who have their hand out for whatever they can get. We say that officers can help to lose that image by applying the methods of promoting to promoting goodwill with the public: Walk into the store and say hello, speak to the children in the park and the old man on the bench, talk to the gas station attendant, the park supervisor, the mailman, the man on the street.

We do not advise our officers to promote gifts or gratuities, but rather we ask them to promote simple friendship. If a man is missing from his job, inquire about his health or his vacation. If a person passes on the street, say hello, do it first, don't wait for others to speak to you. This is the message we give our officers, "Talk to the people."

Obviously there are formal community relation efforts carried

Talk to the People.

out. Police speakers address social or business clubs. Building tours are arranged and traffic safety programs carried out in the schools. All are part of the overall effort.

In the case where there are people of minority races in a community, they should be included as much as possible in the mainstream of the community and they should be included in the number of persons the officer makes it his business to meet and talk with.

In many cases where people of minority groups are asked about their knowledge of their police department, they really know very little. Often the little they do know about the department is colored by exaggeration or outright lies. The only way for people to know the truth is to meet the officers and see for themselves what kind of people serve the city.

In keeping with this idea, officers must be made aware of trigger words that will spark adverse reactions in people, and they must be kept aware of any possible causes for tensions that exist.

Officers are instructed to keep the peace. Emphasis is placed on supressing crime and apprehending criminals. These are basic goals and we must never lose sight of them.

We must also never lose sight of our responsibility to maintain a good working relationship with the citizens for whom we work.

Appearance is important. Just as important is personal behavior of the officer, off and on duty.

A man who drinks to excess, beats his wife and children, or keeps his property in a dirty or disarrayed state is hardly a positive representative of the department. A man who drives his police car too fast, flirts with women, or shirks his duty, is equally poor in his representation of the department.

For this reason it is important to stress personal conduct as a principal responsibility of each man in his role as a representative of the department.

It is our contention that a department which confines the community relations efforts to a limited number of people, and fails to communicate the goals or direction of the program to the entire staff, is missing the boat.

The only way a program of community relations can be successful is to keep all personnel advised what is going on and motivated to support the effort.

Whether a man is assigned to traffic, detectives, or patrol, he is a representative of the department. His performance will affect the lives of community members and his attitude may make or break the community relations of the department.

Chapter 11

RAIDS AND RAIDERS

ONE OF THE MOST difficult subjects upon which the trainer needs to instruct is that of "raids." The subject is particularly and eternally difficult for a number of reasons.

To begin with, not enough people of sufficient rank to draw any water seem to think instruction in the area is at all necessary. Some of them might understand the necessity for such instruction, however, if they were made to think about it. Others, of course, will not agree.

The reason, or one of the reasons, why they will not agree is because they themselves learned the techniques by doing. Since they are likely to be raid leaders, they cannot see the necessity for such instruction.

These allegedly experienced raiders may or may not have been using correct techniques over all of the years. Too, raids are not conducted all *that* frequently. Since it is not really an everyday task, it is one that certainly requires instruction.

The trainer, then, must be armed with sufficient rank and persuasive powers, or perhaps armed with the assistance of rank and influence, with which to convince the Colonel Blimp school as to the necessity of such instruction.

Next, the students will be difficult; for the students, in this case, are of necessity to be drawn from potential raid leaders. Sergeants and detectives are not the easiest students with whom to work. These are singularly self-sufficient people—veteran policemen, leaders and investigators, most of whom have probably either participated in or led raids themselves. In any event, they are not novices, and as such are relatively difficult to instruct.

For all of the foregoing reasons, then, the instructor should himself be an experienced raider who has also read the book. For a book-learned instructor to endeavor to instruct such a group without a background of some practical experience would be ruinous to the program and to the instructor.

"Okay men, here's the plan."

Therefore, the instructors needs to convince the hierarchy as to the need for the instruction; he needs to be able to identify with and relate to the students, in this case experienced policemen. And he needs to know his subject from both the theoretical and the practical standpoints.

The trainer should become an experienced raider, if he is not one already. He can also make use of other officers experienced in raiding.

The trainer should utilize audiovisual aids in this type of instruction, as much as or more so than in any other type of subject matter. Raiding lends to the use of these tools. It may well be that the detective division will have on file photos or tape recordings of raids past, on cases which are past the court appeal stage. Lacking this, the trainer can assemble his own material when he goes a-raiding.

The trainer would do well to cultivate the friendship of the detective boss and/or the patrol tactical commander. This, hopefully will result in his being invited to accompany the raiding party when those occasions and opportunities present themselves. The trainer may go along as a member of the party or as an observer.

In either event, the trainer, without stepping on toes by trying to reorganize raid plans, should endeavor to have the party equipped with any or all of the following: tape recorder, still camera, moving picture camera, videotape recorder. A good raiding party will have some of these tools in any event. Should the trainer find himself having to arrange for the inclusion of the mentioned tools, it may well point up the need for the instruction even then being compiled and prepared.

All such recordings should be tagged, not only by the evidence officer, but by the trainer. Then, when the court case and appeal are over, the trainer will hopefully find the items routed along to him. As a practical matter, however, the trainer should personally follow the case through the various stages and personally stay on the trail of the evidence that is to eventually belong to his training files. Otherwise, he may lose valuable material through the forgetfulness or caprice of the investigating officers.

Definition: A police raid is a sudden attack or invasion of a building or area to effect an apprehension, to secure evidence of illegal activity, or to recover stolen property.

A raid may be planned or it may be spontaneous. In either event, the effectiveness of the raid depends upon the speed with surprise with which it is executed. Some raids may be staged with a minimum of planning and preparation. However, essential factors such as proper coordination and superiority of manpower and firepower must not be overlooked.

The essential factors to be considered in planning the raid are: the mission; the opposition expected, both as to type and strength; the composition of the raiding party; *the orientation of the personnel;* the position and role of each member; the weapons to be carried (in addition to normal sidearms) ; necessary signals; and the evaluation of possible alarm or danger points (a barking dog in the basement of a house nearby the target building, for example) .

The raid plan should be based on sound tactical concepts.

The raid plan should be based on sound tactical concepts. The plan should be adaptable to any contingency. Ornate and overcomplicated raid plans will confuse the personnel and diminish the success ratio of the operation itself. In short, the plan must be simple and elastic.

As his first step in planning, the raid leader will estimate the situation. Then he will make a reconnaissance. It is essential for him to walk over the actual ground, if this can at all be accomplished without aborting the actual raid. Hopefully, also, such reconnaissance can be accomplished legally. However, it is often impractical to go over all of the ground; some of the reconnaissance may of necessity be conducted by camera and binoculars.

Having made his reconnaissance, the leader will then decide upon the signals to be used by his party. His thinking here might include flashlight, whistle, arm and hand signals, a sounding automobile horn.

The transportation plan will now enter his thinking. He may well need, for example, more automobiles returning from the raid than he utilized going to the raid; an accumulation of prisoners resulting from the raid can create this movement problem.

While normal sidearms should always be carried, any given raid might require special weapons. The leader may want to include riflemen from the antisniper team, and/or men who are well drilled in the use of tear smoke. Should the estimate of the situation and the reconnaissance of the ground indicate the probability of a fire fight, then the leader will carefully lay out the fields of fire for his men. This is a twofold problem; he will want to bring superior firepower to bear, and he will want to avoid his men being hit by "friendly" fire. In every instance, special weapons should be assigned only to men who have displayed familiarity and proficiency with those weapons. Training files may be of use here; without this, oftentimes the raiders are more in danger from their fellows than they are from the bad guys.

Having studied the situation and formulated his plan, the leader will then anticipate all possible contingencies, and have alternate, but simple, plans formulated for those contingencies.

The orientation of the raiding party is key to the entire program. It is the stage that is more often either ignored or flubbed than any other. It is essential that the entire raiding party be present for orientation. Too often, uniform men, detailed to aid a detective type raid, are merely "brought along" as additional or replacement personnel, and are not really considered an integral part of the raiding team.

To repeat, *all* involved personnel must be briefed, and briefed together. This is even more so when more than one agency are involved in the raid. This is essential to teamwork, and is a preventive to the raiders shooting each other.

The leader must be an experienced raider. He will appoint other experienced raiders as assistant raid leader and as team leaders. Having done this, he will assign every member of the raiding party to a unit of the party. Mostly, these will fall into three categories: the covering party, the entering party, and the prisoner guard.

The leader, or his designate, will then orient the raiders. Each man's role will be explained to him and to the group in specifics. Each man then should always be required to recite back each specific of his assignment in order to establish and signify complete understanding by all hands. Again, this is essential, and it is the thing that is most often fouled up. The leader should avoid playing "God"; at this point his work in planning is finished, for he only (only!) needs to lead the raid; he needs verbal participation from his people in order to ensure that communication has taken place. In this fashion, he will avoid miscues at the raid scene.

It is at this session that the blueprint of the raid should be unveiled to the raiders. Here is the time to use a scale model, or perhaps a sand table. Maps, photos, sketches and diagrams are most valuable for this session. This can all be put into perspective by use of a "chalk talk," just as before the football game.

The chalk talk should cover the general area, the terrain, and the buildings, both exterior and interior. Can the raiders expect any doors to be unlocked? Because a man is armed with a sledgehammer and a desire to go through the door assigned to him is no reason for him not to try the doorknob first. Doors are often left unlocked. It is easier and quicker to go through a door by means of doorknob vis a vis the sledge. This is not to suggest that the sledge should not be used. It should be used, well and with alacrity by an experienced sledge man if the door is locked and it does not appear that the people inside are about to open up.

The chalk talk should point up entrances and exits, and windows, both to be covered and those to be utilized to get in. Adjunct to this are the points of cover and concealment, which include the avenues of approach by the raiders.

If the raid is nocturnal in nature, then lighting is an element of concern. What and where with respect to street lights? Do we use spotlights, flashlights, or other forms of illumination?

Communications, both between the raiders, and between raider and he who is about to be raided are to be covered here. Handi-talkie radios, for example, should have been charged and checked before now, and should be issued at this point.

At the chalk talk, every member of the raiding party will learn the location of every element of the party, whether or not he will have any planned contact with those elements.

The delineation of roadblock points are done at this time. Roadblocks are important to the plan, as a means of keeping the suspect(s) inside and the public outside of the area to be attacked.

Avenues and means of escape are thoroughly covered at the chalk talk. The possible warning devices, including that barking dog, that have been discovered during the initial and subsequent reconnaissances, will be delineated for the raiders. This is the time, also, to explain the fields of fire assigned to the men.

Between the all-important orientation and the actual execution of the raid, *it is essential to keep all raiders together!* No man can be allowed even a mundane trip to the men's room unaccompanied. It is not time to go out for a cup of coffee. This is true of all raids, and even more so when more than one agency is involved.

The reason for this supercaution has to do with security; security of the men's safety; security of the operation itself; *security of the fact that a raid is set to go down at all anywhere;* and last, but far, far from least, security against the possible charge of a real or imagined tipoff. This is all basic and most essential; it is an area that is easily and frequently disregarded; it is a matter about which the leader must be very hardnosed, and which should be made a part of his orientation. The breaking of this rule should result in immediate negative discipline and the future exclusion of the culprit from raiding parties.

The execution of the raid involves the approach, the check at the rendevous, and the actual operation. A guard is to be left for vehicles. The slamming of car doors is a no-no. When the group is in position, predetermined signals are implemented so that everybody knows that everybody is set.

If it is the type of raid wherein the raiders will communicate with the persons about to be raided, it is at this point that that communication is used. This may be, and probably will be, required legally (as in the search warrant situation). Legalistics and good tactics do not always go hand in hand, to make an extreme understatement. Therefore, the sledge men (or the man with the key, or the doorknob man) must be told to move off fast.

Then, when the legalistics are complied with by telephone, public address system, or the knock on the door, they must move aggressively and quickly. Time is of the essence, the door will be gotten through *now;* then the entering party moves, fast, to preassigned locations in the now familiar mission. While the officers must be "legal," they must be as aggressive and direct as possible commensurate with that aura of legality. This is necessary for the safety of the men, the efficiency of the operation, and the successful attainment of the goal. The predesignated reporting and evidence officers will later in court be prepared to prove legality by their testimony and other evidence.

With the raid completed in terms of taking prisoners and securing the area, when it is safe, then is the time to be concerned with investigative efficiency. Surplus men should be grouped nearby, and in some cases returned to other duties. With the area mostly cleared, photographic, investigative, and evidentiary efforts are carried out professionally and efficiently. As evidence is found in the room by room search, for example, it should not be seized; it should instead be called to the attention of the evidence officer who will properly record location of the find and mark, label, and store it all himself. This simplifies later court testimony.

At the conclusion of the entire raid is the time to regroup the raiders and call the roll. Roll call is as necessary here as it is at the orientation. The leader needs to determine that all of his men are there, that no one is lying, injured or dead, in the alley. It is also a precaution against the oversight of leaving some faithful policeman stand on an overlooked and now unnecessary, post hour after hour.

The leader will also determine at this stage whether it is necessary to leave guards when the main party clears the area. The necessity for this assignment is dependent upon the need to guard evidence or seize and arrest returning accomplices.

A partial checklist of raid equipment follows: revolvers; shoulder weapons (shotguns, rifles, gas guns, flare guns); ammunition (ball, tracer, tear smoke); grenades (smoke, marker, tear smoke); flares (signal, illumination); transportation (types, amount); communication (radio, whistle, public address system, signal lights, megaphones, dimes for pay telephones); lights (flashlights, spotlights, sniperscopes); time pieces (radium dials to work on inside of wrists); gas masks; restraining devices, first aid kits; cameras (movie, still, videotape recorders, audio recorders); tools for entry (sledges, axes, crowbars, keys).

We suggest that the training officer sell the need for instruction in the raid area. He should assemble his instructional material and his assistant instructors. Both material and instructors should be heavily supplied with audiovisual aids.

Then the trainer should become an experienced raider, if he is not already qualified. Instruction comes next; part of the instruction is the critique after every raid. New problems and techniques can then be injected into the future and, hopefully, continuing instruction on raids.

Finally, the trainer needs to record his efforts. A file of trained and experienced raiders can and should be maintained, and continuously updated. The file should be located (duplicated, triplicated) in the training division, Chief's office, and in a centrally located skills file, where this and other skills are listed.

Chapter 12

PREPARING FOR ROLL CALL TRAINING

Most police agencies carry on some form or "roll call training." In many cases the programs are not doing the job.

The lessons, generally delivered during or following briefing, are usually about ten minutes in length. This is hardly enough time to deliver a lengthy message, or bring about a major change in procedures.

We feel there are many lessons that can be taught in such a time period, if care is taken to properly prepare the lessons and the trainers.

It is an insult to the men for a supervisor to walk into the room and read from a lesson plan he has never before looked at.

It is also very poor taste for a supervisor to provide "editorial" comment about a lesson with which he does not agree.

If you carry on a program of this type, provide the trainers with copies of the lessons in advance of the time they are to present them. Provide ample time for the supervisors to read and understand the material. Such provision also makes it possible for them to challenge anything they might feel is incorrect or improper.

It may be that there needs to be more explanation of what is behind the lesson. Perhaps the reason for change is not fully explained, and therefore the supervisors fail to feel they can support the lesson.

In the situation where there is some major objection, or objection by several people, we recommend that the lesson be withdrawn, at least until there can be a meeting with the people who must carry out the delivery of the message. The problems should be thoroughly explored, and the lesson plan modified, if necessary to make the situation clear.

If the watch supervisors are conducting the training, they should be at the station in advance of the men, and prepared, not only to deliver the lesson, but to answer any questions that arise.

From time to time, the training officer should attend the roll call and observe how the lessons are delivered, and whether the supervisors are prepared.

If there is any problem in this area, the watch commander should be solicited to coordinate with the training officer and eliminate the difficulty.

As with any other training material, there should be some evaluation of how well the men are receiving and understanding the information.

In some cases this is accomplished by checking how well they carry out the task that is the subject of the lesson. In other cases, the supervisors should ask questions, either formally, at roll call, or informally, when they meet with their men in the street.

If the information is not getting across, the program must be improved to carry out the mission.

"That's not the film we had scheduled!"

The roll call is often the place where video tapes, or motion pictures are shown. If this is to be done, the supervisor must prepare the equipment in advance of the arrival of the men and be prepared to begin with little delay.

The projectionist should be in position. The necessary information to be covered in roll call should be dealt with as quickly as possible and the film should begin.

Many films require more than the time usually allowed for such training. If that is the case, arrangements must be made for someone to cover the street as the film is shown.

When such a film is on the schedule, provision must be made to show it on all watches, and for several days. This provides an opportunity for all men to view the film.

A record should be kept indicating which personnel have viewed the presentation. The training time should be reported to the Chief for his records.

Do not assume that a lesson is understood and well received because no questions are asked. Take the initiative to seek out the men to find out if they understand.

One word of caution, be sure your program is suitable for classroom delivery. You can't teach men to shoot by talking about it, nor will they learn to march by discussing it.

Obviously there may be some aspect of such training that requires classroom lectures, but for the largest part, there must be physical participation to make such programs pay off, and at roll call is not the place for this kind of training.

If the trainer understands his limitations, the roll call program can be a true asset to your training program.

PART IV

IN-SERVICE TRAINING

Chapter 13

INSTRUCTING

T HE ACT of teaching involves more than just telling someone how to do something. Some instructors unconsciously utilize proper techniques, while some who are trained to instruct just do not make good instructors.

Essentially, the police training officer is an instructor. He is many other things, too, including a coordinator, a leader, an example, a policeman still, and so on. He is in essence an instructor nonetheless. Should he head up a large training division, he will need subordinate instructors. Thus, even if he no longer instructs very often, he may well have to instruct his instructors on how to instruct.

In the case listed, he may want to have his instructors read this chapter. This chapter comments on instruction.

The simplest explanation of teaching we know sums it all up admirably. "Tell 'em what you are going to tell 'em; then tell 'em; then tell 'em what you told 'em." This is very good advice. Of course, it is broad advice, and should be filled in with a few details. The instructor should continue to come back to the basic advice, however, even after mastering the other details and skills of instructing.

There are five steps an instructor should follow. This is true whether he is teaching for a full semester in a junior college or teaching a two hour class in report writing.

The instructor prepares his lesson. He presents the material to the class. He causes the students to apply what they have learned. He conducts an examination to ascertain that they have learned their lesson. He holds a discussion in the classroom and a critique in the field.

In preparing his lesson, the instructor must first ascertain where and when he is to hold his class. This sounds rather too basic, but schedules and time slots do not always coincide nicely; too, there are schedule changes from time to time, and he should check just in the event he didn't get the word.

The instructor will determine the objective of his lesson, and through analysis will try to tie in his material into things of which the students are already knowledgeable. Audio and visual aids should be decided upon at this point, whether or not to use, and which will be utilized if so.

He will review his array of sea stories to determine which, if any, are appropriate to use as examples of points being made. A story is a good method of launching into the subject matter at the beginning of the lesson. A caution: as stated elsewhere herein, stories are valuable for example and illustration, to show realities that result from the theoretical matters being taught; no classroom session should consist entirely of war stories—that is not instructing. Stories are tools and examples, used to make points, and are not the substitute for other and basic teaching techniques.

An outline of the presentation can be made at this point. Included in the outline should be the method which the instructor intends to use in order to make his point. Also to be written in are test questions, problems, and assignments to be made, if any. A list of reference material, including suggested and optional readings will complete this list and is a valuable adjunct to the instructional period (s) .

A rehearsal is in order for an instructor. This is particularly so if the instructor is new, or if he is about to introduce material that he has not instructed upon before.

As with rehearsing for a speech, the bedroom mirror is valuable to this effort. Facial expressions and hand gestures can be studied first hand by the instructor. An acquiescent spouse might consent to listen and watch rehearsal, and to comment critically. This is not always best for conjugal tranquillity, however.

Rehearsal before an officer or officers of like or higher rank is the most valuable rehearsal method. It allows the instructor to give his complete class, just as he would in the classroom, before an audience that will be understanding, knowledgeable, and unafraid to employ the necessary criticism.

The instructor should check the physical scene, the classroom, his supply of chalk, and any and all audio and visual aids that he will use. An extra bulb for the motion picture projector is in order, for example. Do battery operated devices have charged batteries? Has the proper reel of film arrived?

Presentation commences with the arrival of the instructor at the classroom site. The instructor should always be early—a fifteen minute head start usually seems about right. If the room is unoccupied at this time, then the instructor has this time in which to assemble his materials and equipment. He can at this point, if he prefers, make early notations on the chalk board. He will not, however, want to display so much material as to distract the attention of his class.

Of course, if the students are in the classroom for a previous period of instruction, the newly arrived instructor should wait courteously for his predecessor to complete his presentation. The presence of the newly arrived man will remind the "old" instructor that his time is almost up. If he weren't already aware of the fact, he is now and can begin to sum up.

All classes should have a ten minute break between the end

of one and beginning of the next. The instructor can utilize this ten minutes to make the arrangements previously described. It is important that the instructor be present prior to the classtime. He lends his "presence" to the scene early, and this tends to help him establish control of the class. If the class is a police academy class, and there is an officer assigned to lead the class, or if there is a class monitor, then the instructor's task is somewhat eased in this sense.

He needs to be certain that each man has a seat and that each man is present. The leader or monitor will usually do this job; where there are neither leader nor monitor, the instructor should ascertain that several seating charts are available to assist the students. Should there be no seat assignments, then the instructor's presence early will indeed help him to establish control.

The men will tend to sit to the rear of the classroom. Should the instructor allow this prior to his asking them to sit up front, he has lost that small amount of control, and added some confusion to the beginning of the class. The resulting movement is always somewhat disruptive. He does better to meet the class as they enter the room, and to politely insist they fill up the front rows of seats first.

The class should always be started promptly. Roll call is important. The instructor reads a name and awaits an affirmative answer. A nonanswer means the man is absent. Reasons for absence should be checked later. It is possible, perhaps even probable, that the absentee is "in court" as the result of a subpoena. It is also possible that this favorite policeman's excuse for absence is just that, an excuse. After class, it behooves the instructor to ascertain whether the man was in fact in court—and what time he was released from court, if he was.

Having checked those present, he does well to count the names listed as present against the number of bodies in the classroom. On occasion there will be more names checked as present than there are people present. It is another old game, and it should never happen more than once to the same instructor. A leader or monitor will usually keep this down. In an academy class, disciplinary action might well result from this malfeasance. Usually, it is most effective for the instructor, without comment, to quietly repeat the roll call. The class will get the message.

The instructor does better to talk to (and with) his students, and not through the window, to a wall or his notes or at the ceiling.

A little nervousness or stage fright prior to a class might be more usual than it is unusual. An instructor, particularly if he is not a veteran instructor, should expect this. It is another reason for proper preparation and rehearsal. The man who is properly prepared can carry on in spite of nervousness. This is a theory of combat shooting, for example. In that case, proper drill overcomes a natural nervousness in a life or death situation.

A routine thing accomplished will somewhat ease this natural tenseness. Perhaps this is a good time to write on the chalkboard, and then launch into the lesson. To ask a good question of the class right off will get things going while helping the instructor to master his uneasiness and the students.

The lecture should be introduced by telling the students what you are going to tell them. A good introduction will take about ten percent of the allotted class time. An introduction should tie in the lesson with things the class has already learned. An attention-getting applicable anecdote is well placed at the beginning of the introduction.

A lecture is valuable to present several ideas to a group. Generally a lecture should be used to introduce or to sum up topics. It is useful to explain a demonstration; but it is limited to the sense of hearing. The students receive only what they hear—the other senses remain unaffected. Therefore, lectures should be short. Fifteen or twenty minutes are about right, unless and until audio or visual aids are added to the presentation.

The students have been told what they are going to be told. Now the instructor should tell them. The instructor will tell the students why he and they are there. In a moderate voice, loud enough for all to hear, using language understandable to the students, the instructor will: motivate and challenge the group, use their language, utilize proper gestures, maintain his poise and emphasize the important points. He talks directly to the students at all times.

He can utilize his notes by looking at them from time to time, never surreptitiously. He should not, however, either memorize his presentation or read from a prepared paper.

The instructor should stand erect, balanced with feet slightly apart. His hands are available for illustrative gestures; the hands do not belong in pockets nor should they be utilized as a windmill. He should stand reasonably still. Like the voice, hand gestures should be studied and moderate, with emphasis added when a strong point must be made.

Student participation in the form of class discussion is an excellent instructional technique. With the guidance of the instructor, the students are thus helped to think out their own answers to the problems at hand.

The instructor commences the discussion with a story, an example or a question. Having started the students thinking about the question, he then throws them the ball. With guidance and control from the instructor, the students do most of the talking. It is a mistake for the discussion leader to "expert." Gentle probes and questions from him will keep the discussion going. When the class leaves the track, he must get them back on the track, of course.

Questions of fact should be answered by the instructor; this is so even if the lecture has covered the point. The student who has missed the point, if he is acting in good faith, deserves a straight answer. It is possible that others in the class have also missed the point, but have been too shy to ask. Thus, the instructor gives the answer, impartially and without hostility.

Other questions, however, should be answered by the class. The instructor answers question with question, throwing back the ball in each case. He encourages all to participate, sometimes by direct question, other times by asking the nonparticipant whether he agrees or disagrees with someone's answer or thought.

Questions by the instructor should be thought-provoking to the class. With the lecture or discussion ended, the instructor should approach questions in a positive manner. "Are there any questions?" Pause. No questions, perhaps. Then, "All right, I'll ask a few questions." Then a question of the class, clear and succinct. Pause. The class is thinking. Then the instructor can call on a member of the class. To call a man by name and then to ask the question is to turn off the rest of the class.

When students ask a question of the instructor, they deserve an answer. Should the instructor not know the answer, he should never try to bluff—he will lose the respect and confidence of his class. He should tell the class that he does not know, that he will find out and let them know, *and he should find out and let them know!*

Handout material is an important study aid. Such material should be handed out at the end of a session. This prevents a diminution of attention by students starting to read the material during the lecture or discussion. Handouts should give source credit. It is helpful as an attention getter for the material to be pleasing to the eye. Sloppy material is worthless, for the students will not read it. Since students hopefully receive an abundance of handouts, the instructor does well to have his on colored paper, a different color, if possible, for each of his handouts. The student is much more likely to peruse that which is well made up and pleasing to the eye.

Audio training aids are an excellent supplement to a lecture. As noted elsewhere in these writings, a tape recording of a raid, and indeed even of the instruction prior to and the critique following the raid, is a practical and entertaining adjunct to a class on raids. And so on with other classes. Tape recordings are particularly valuable for classes on interview and interrogation, and are fine illustrations regarding the admonishments of rights situation.

Visual aids are valuable because they apply to the sense of sight. The lecture is reinforced because the students are now being "assailed" via two senses, those of sight and hearing. Charts, diagrams, and photographs are included here, in addition to chalkboard sketches, film strips, sand tables, models, mock ups, and the like.

A little imagination on the part of the instructor will produce workable and realistic visual aids. Take the matter of the sand table (for that matter, should a raid be the subject, a flat table will suffice). The instructor can easily erect wooden or cardboard box buildings. He can chalk-line in streets. Toy automobiles and toy soldiers, available at the nearest toy store, dime store or son's home toy box work admirably as models for this purpose.

Training films (motion pictures) are becoming ever more available to, in and from law enforcement. The instructor in each case *must* personally review the film prior to showing it to his class. Thus, he not only ascertains that he has the correct film (we really should not confront a class of Block Parent Mothers, present to learn something of burglary prevention, with a sneak preview on "The Treatment of Venereal Disease!"), but he learns what is out of date in the film. The film may still be valuable; the instructor needs to be prepared to comment on discrepancies or out of date practices or obsolete equipment portrayed on the screen.

Videotape recordings, television, can and does allow for the employment of everything mentioned in this chapter thus far. It is an excellent training device. All of the instructional wiles and devices herein discussed can easily be rehearsed and portrayed. All that need be added is the presence of the instructor to answer questions, to question, and perhaps to lead the discussion. (See *Closed Circuit Television for Police,* Hansen and Kolbmann, Charles C Thomas, Publisher.)

Application is learning by doing. Here the students endeavor to practice that which has been taught them by the instructor. Here the instructor must pay particularly strict attention to his students. It is difficult for a man to unlearn anything, once learned. Hence, he must determine that his charges do the thing correctly the first time, and then to repeat and repeat until the application phase of the instruction is completed. Rote, or repetitive, training still has value.

Application lends itself to the Coach-Pupil method. Two students, paired off, assume and occasionally reverse the roles. This form of application works extremely well in marksmanship and first aid classes. It is also valuable in search and self-defense classes.

The military has made good use of the field problem in training. There is no reason why the police cannot do likewise. One of the authors conducted a field problem in surveillance in a crowded shopping center, using a class of some thirty plus people. It was most successful, inasmuch as unforseen problems and mistakes occurred, just as they do in the real thing.

Examination may be verbal and/or written. Written exams can be of the essay, fill-in, true-false, or matching type. Written exams should be tested for validity and applicability prior to being given to students. Neither student nor instructor should be judged by the results of a single test. However, the instructor who never has a student fail, and he who has most or all of his students fail, is a failure as an instructor.

The instructor's task is to impart knowledge to the students. Let it be so.

Chapter 14

TRAINING FOR SPECIAL SERVICES

T HE BACKBONE of the police department is the patrol force and for this reason the largest part of this book deals with training uniformed personnel.

We have included a chapter on "Raids" in this writing. Raids are generally carried out by nonuniformed people, detectives.

We submit that every good police officer is not necessarily a good detective. However, a good officer with proper training can be an asset. The experience he gains from working as a detective can greatly expand his knowledge in the field.

In our recommended schedule of recruit training we included orientation to the detective's role. If an officer is to work as a detective, we recommend greatly expanded training in this area. Some departments favor training assignments as a program for this need.

A training assignment in the nonuniform services should be closely supervised and directed. The man should be assigned to work each area for a period, to become familiar with the importance of follow-up investigation, and to give him an overview of the problems. During the assignment he should work with experienced detectives in order that he might study their methods.

There is a distinct difference in the reactions of the public to a detective as opposed to a uniformed officer. There is also generally more individual responsibility placed on the detective.

The trainee learns the importance of planning his work to the best advantage.

As each area is covered in the training, the officer expands his knowledge of the specialized techniques needed, and he gets a personal view of how the experienced detectives work.

Another benefit of such on the job training is the exposure to officers from other departments with whom a detective must work.

There is much to be learned from the professional detective and we recommend this kind of program both as a training ground for people who are to be assigned as detectives and for the benefit of all officers possible.

As a side benefit of such a program, trainees often meet informants who deal with detectives and are able to deal with them in future contacts. We are not suggesting a practice of "poaching" informants. It is quite possible, though that some informants can, and will, work with several officers.

Another special service area often neglected is communnications. Many communications employees are civilians and for some reason chiefs take the position that they do not need the same intensified training as officers.

We agree that in some areas dispatchers or clerical employees do not need training. In others, such training is essential.

A dispatcher who has little first hand knowledge of what street police work is all about can make tragic mistakes that can endanger the officers.

Before a dispatcher is left in the radio room alone, he must be thoroughly schooled to understand the constant danger that exists on the street. He must know the importance of instant response to calls from the radio, and he must be taught to evaluate calls for service and help that come from the citizens.

As a part of his training, we recommend assigning a dispatcher to ride as an observer for a period, to see for himself what it is like. He should be rotated to work all watches, and all areas of the city.

Care should be taken to point out "hot spots" and he should note them for future reference.

This exposure gives him some idea of the physical layout of the city and a first-hand view of how the public reacts to the police officer.

Most departments have rules governing the duties and requirements of dispatchers and other civilians employed in the organization.

To explain the responsibilities and the regulations as they relate to the man's job is important. He should also be made to understand the functions of the officers, and their responsibilities.

If a dispatcher is trained on the job, he should be rotated to all watches, and made basically familiar with the workings of each.

It is a common practice for dispatchers to be trained on the day watch, and then assigned to a night detail "fully trained."

This is absurd. There are distinct variances between day and night police departments. In such a situation the man must be trained to handle those unique problems he will face.

The Policemachine.

In this day of automation, dispatchers or clerical employees are required to work with complex computors or communications equipment. Often, they are the only persons trained in the use of the sophisticated machinery.

We contend that supervisory personnel must also be trained in this area, and a number of officers as well.

It is common in the medium-sized department for one or two dispatchers to work on a watch. If vacations or illness remove those people, someone must do the job.

Additionally, if supervisors are not trained in the basic functions of the equipment, how can they evaluate the performance of their personnel.

"Here it is. Get to work."

No one should be allowed to underestimate the importance of the dispatcher. He is the officer's life-line in emergency and the citizen's link to our services. Neither can afford incompetence in the job.

We assume that all departments teach their personnel telephone courtesy and the routine business functions they need and we will not cover those areas in this writing.

There are many other "special" service areas in law enforcement, traffic safety, warrant service, technical services, and others.

Take the initiative to establish sound guidelines for each of these areas and train your people adequately before expecting them to perform the job.

As we noted, a training officer is not created by handing down a title. Neither is a dispatcher, or a technician, or a detective created by proclamation. The responsibility lies with the Chief to support and train his men to do the job.

We are of the opinion that such programs are properly under the guidance of the training division. We are equally aware that such special training may involve people working in other divisions, because of the nature of the information and experience needed to carry out the mission.

For this reason we note the training officer must maintain a good working relationship with others within the department and solicit their willing participation in training efforts.

Compliance with an order from the chief requiring their assistance in training is something that can be obtained. Cooperation and the extras that go into a positive program are something else.

We have all read stories of machines taking over the world, or becoming the masters of their inventors. Consider how easy it would be to create our own "monster" by letting our technical knowledge of the computers and similar aids fall behind.

We have a vast number of excellent tools in such programs as NCIC, CLETS, PIN, AUTOSTATIS, SMARTS,* and all the other mysterious banks of knowledge with which we are equipped.

By failing to adequately train sufficient personnel, we create the "indispensible man." If only one man or a few men in the department have this knowledge, they become a sort of special power group.

---

*National Crime Information Center, California Law Enforcement Teletype System, Police Information Network AUTOmatic STatewide Auto Theft Inquiry System, San Mateo Automatic Radio Teletype System.

We recommend training some policemen to do the jobs of the civilians. We also have suggested training civilians in some of the work of the officers for their better knowledge of their jobs. We suggest, whenever possible, you combine these groups for classes that will benefit both. There is the obvious benefit of economy in such a move, and by having the men become better acquainted they will have a more personal interest in each others problems.

We are not pointing this chapter at any specific problems, but rather giving some examples of areas we feel have been neglected.

Each department has some unique program or problem that must be dealt with. We simply suggest that you attack the problems from the point of view of training and the problem may become less as the knowledge of the workers becomes greater.

The one point we feel we must make is that whenever an officer is assigned to some special detail for training, the training division must be kept advised of his progress and his performance. This data should be reported in writing and maintained in the man's personnel folder.

We also offer a word of caution concerning the selection of trainers in special programs such as we have described.

There are men who are adept at their work, and who have developed certain personal techniques that work well for them. It is wrong to let such a man train an inexperienced person. The uninitiated worker may learn how to get a result by the method, without ever knowing why it comes out the way it does, or the meaning of the job.

A program should include all the phases of the operation if it is to be meaningful. There should be some written guidelines of areas to be covered and the guide should be adhered to. There should be ample time for questions and a time to apply the lessons that have been learned.

Chapter 15

REFRESHER TRAINING PROGRAMS

T RAINING for law enforcement personnel cannot stop with the basic training period. We must be prepared to refresh or reinforce training by frequent introduction of new methods or procedures.

Among the most critical areas in this regard is changes in legislation and court decisions.

It seems that every time we adjust to a new court policy someone in a higher court reverses a decision, or extends a previous decision that makes it necessary for us to change again.

We saw this happen with the noted Dorado and Escobedo cases, and we see it with great frequency in issues concerning searches.

We learn to overcome the natural resentment of the officers at the constant changes. To better establish the purpose of new procedures we must offer some explanation of the case.

This explanation will best come in the form of a brief of the case, and the decision, providing the officers with insight to how the decision was reached.

The training officer may obtain the information from law bulletins, or better, from his district attorney. In presenting this information, there must be care to present the case in as unbiased a manner as possible. We grant that some decisions make our work more difficult. We also know that we have no choice but to abide by the decisions and therefore we must strive to find any positive aspects we can, and make the law work for us.

Your lessons may take the form of information bulletins to be presented and circulated to the men. Or, they may take the form of personal lectures or video-tapes delivered by a member of the district attorney's staff.

In such delivery, there will be less room for argument by those who are hard to change, and the officers will be taught to operate in the manner the prosecutor feels will be most effective.

The result should be less danger of having cases lost in court on technical points, and a better relationship between the police and the prosecutor.

We note that actual changes in written law are much less frequent than the changes wrought by court decision. Still, this area must be covered in our training.

Every department should be obtaining legislative bulletins covering new laws and changes in existing laws, prior to the time the laws go into effect.

Prior to that time, the officers should be briefed on the law and some statement of department policy established and released to all hands.

Another area of training that is neglected is that of review or refresher training in technical areas.

In many cases there is never a retraining period offered and officers forget lessons they were taught as recruits.

Some areas such as first aid, use of chemical agents, and others are reviewed because of requirements to obtain certificates, or because of association with some other training exercise.

Most other areas are not reviewed, and often because of lack of application, the officers lose their proficiency.

There are some benefits to bringing in experienced officers to specific classes in recruit training. It is good review for the veterans, and the recruits often learn a great deal from the experience of the others.

We note that the assignment to such classes should not be made in such a way that the veteran officers are demeaned in any way. Review should not be regarded as indicating a lack of knowledge, or performance, and care should be taken to make all the officers understand that.

We do not recommend having large numbers of veterans in classes with recruits at one time. They tend to overwhelm the recruits who may hesitate to ask questions for fear of looking stupid.

In some cases the veteran officer may be recruited to review the course by acting as an assistant to the instructor.

When new procedures are developed requiring some skills

beyond those of a recruit or new officer, or information of an advanced nature is to be distributed, lessons should be prepared in a manner to relate the new material to existing knowledge. The lessons should also be prepared in such a manner as to be directed at experienced personnel, and at an appropriate level.

It is not proper to expect experienced officers to sit through the same basic training classes they took as recruits, unless something can obviously be gained by doing so.

If a man has shown an ignorance of a particular subject, then it is proper to train him. If there have been significant changes in an area this would be appropriate.

It would not be proper to have experienced men assigned to the entire recruit program.

In many cases it will be convenient to have refresher classes involving small groups of officers, in other cases you may need to gather many men together for such classes. In either case, plan your lessons, and arrange your time and facilities as you would for any other training class.

PART V

TRAINING FOR PROMOTION AND SUPERVISORS

Chapter 16

PREPARATION FOR WRITTEN EXAMINATIONS

IN TERMS OF WRITTEN examinations, the police training officer is primarily concerned with promotional examinations. Any interest on his part in entrance examinations, as they affect his department, are strictly ancillary and peripheral to his main interest and mission.

This is not to say that the trainer need not encourage and counsel interested potential candidates who ask for advice. It is to say he is not an employment officer. Encouragement to the candidate for entrance is gentlemanly, compassionate, and professional. His official time and main effort should be with the men who already are departmental members. His debt to them is that they are *here now* and he is their trainer.

While there is not a superabundance of promotional positions available in police work, there is an abundance of candidates. The law of supply and demand applies to the extent that the supply is much greater than the demand.

Some of the candidates sincerely wish to become leaders—patrolmen to be sergeants, sergeants to be lieutenants, and so on. Others take the tests for a lark or as a challenge, with no clear idea as to why they are taking it, or as to whether they would accept the position if offered. Still others, unfortunately, take the test to obtain a pay raise. We say "unfortunately" because these men do not desire and would rather not have the responsibility of the leader—and they will not be true leaders even if appointed. The police structure mostly does not allow for advancement, pay raises per se, save for annual cost of living adjustments and through promotionals, almost all of which have to do with supervision. It is an evil of the system. This is changing, slowly, and the change will continue in the future.

Some dedicated and ambitious policemen are self-starters, who

119

will attend school and involve themselves in home study. A truly serious man can easily spend one to two years of home study for a promotional examination. To do this they will sacrifice some or all of their social life. The man who sacrifices none of his social life in this situation is either extremely bright or is foredoomed to fail his test. Psychologically, some of these use the excuse of a nagging wife to "take out" as an excuse for insufficient study and the resultant failure in the promotional examination. They really didn't want to be sergeants.

The police training officer can assist the officers in a course of study and in the development of study habits. He can encourage the officers, and aid them as they request. He should set up a course of study, probably for one year minimum, and introduce each interested officer to the same course of study. He must not be accused of playing favorites; contrariwise, he can and should ethically assist any man as much as that man requests and so long as that man is producing, both on the job and in his studies.

We say the trainer should establish a one year study regimen. Realistically, numerous officers do not commence to study until the examination announcement is posted. Then, a flurry of apprehension and activity. Officers who logically should have been studying all along are now questioning, surmising, rumor mongering, and borrowing study material from others who purchased the material. It is illogical and incongruous, but that is the way it is. The trainer, thus, should also have prepared a "short course" of study. This is the one that precludes and eliminates most of the reading material. It is essentially a test-taking type of study, which is essentially the last phase of the long-course of study.

Study, as we have indicated, starts a minimum of one year prior to the promotional examination. To set up his course of study, the trainer must first research. He should study the testing system. Are the tests provided from outside agencies, from his own police department or personnel office, where? If possible to obtain, he should peruse old test copies; he should be familiar with the general thrust of the particular exam (sergeant, lieutenant) from that particular agency.

He will amass material from coaching schools and publishers.

"Here's the material to study for the Sergeant test. Better get started."

He will have on hand brochures and order blanks, so that his people can spend their money where it will do them the most good. He should have complete files on this, so that he can assist the officers at any time in this fashion, and not only when an exam is imminent.

Some jurisdictions provide for the listing of books from which test questions will be extracted. When and where this does not occur, the trainer hopefully will be able to cause it to occur. He should at least be able to publish a list of books to study. When the chips are not yet down, and the exam not yet announced, the trainer should see that this group of publications, and others, are available to the officers through the police training library. Once the exam is announced, officers may have to borrow or buy the appropriate books from that list. The police library at this point should probably have the books available on a reading room basis only, so as to benefit the most officers, and to preclude any one or two candidates from tying the books up.

The long range, or at least long, reading program is essential to the studying officer. The trainer will advise and encourage the applicant to continue his reading up to the closing days of the course of study.

Other than police reading should occur. Personnel and management matters are written upon in many fields in addition to the police field, for example. Study of police community relations can be assisted by perusal of sociological works and governmental studies, for example. Police works per se should not, of course, be neglected.

The trainer does well to ascertain that his people can in fact read. What is their reading comprehension? Tests have reading comprehension sections. Multiple choice tests are often difficult to read, in addition. Officers will know the answers to some questions, and will not know the answers to others. Too often, however, the candidate will not properly read, or will not properly comprehend the meaning of the question itself. How often this?: "I could have answered had I been able to understand the question."

Logically, then, the trainer can himself test for reading comprehension. He can train his people in this in other ways. Encouragement to read other than usual material is most helpful. The officer should be touted onto sections of the newspaper that he does not normally read. Even in this day of women's liberation, most newspapers have a woman's page. A forced reading of the woman's Page, for example, exposes the candidate to unusual, for him, reading. Questions by the officer's wife will later establish what he has attained from that reading. A nightly/daily repetition of the ritual will assist his reading comprehension.

Eventually, the students get down to the wire. In the last month or two, prior to the actual exam, comes the time to test and practice at testing. In the case of the above mentioned late-starting candidates, this becomes the primary phase of their short course preparation.

The course of time will tend to provide the training officer with various multiple choice examinations. Some will just come to him, others will emanate from his own police academy and courses of instruction. When and where possible, past exams from the jurisdiction should be saved and appropriately filed. Coaching schools are in the business of testing, and tests can be purchased from those endeavors.

The trainer can set up his own coaching school (not private enterprise; should be accomplished within departmental framework). He can assemble his voluntary class and explain theories and procedures.

"A question which says 'always' or 'never' usually should receive a negative answer."

"Don't hang up on a difficult question. Skip it, finish, and come back to the question if time allows. It is better to miss one question than several."

"Practice and practice, repeat and repeat. Learn the mechanics of testing as well as the right answers."

"You are usually looking for, not necessarily the positively correct answer, but for the *most nearly correct answer*."

"Reading comprehension—practice it, live with it. What is the question really asking? If you can't comprehend the question, you can't give the correct answer."

"Do not read into the question. The simplest and clearest meaning of the question is what you are looking for."

"Then, test and retest, in class and at home. Retake the same tests, take all available tests."

The student should not try to correct his own examinations;

it is bad psychologically and poor for morale. Someone else should correct the student's practice examinations while he takes yet other exams. The instructor or an aide will do this in class, a wife or friend at home. All time should be spent either testing or checking incorrect answers so that they are not missed the next time around.

The Trainer should convince and encourage the student at this point in time to forego all other efforts save on-duty problems. If possible, the student should take some time off the job. At all events, the student should spend all waking nonworking hours at his testing.

Be ready.

The trainer should try to peak his student at the end of the study course. He will have his candidates cease heavy study the day before the exam. Some small amount of review is all the student need do at this point. It is too late to learn anything new. Then, a relaxed evening at home, early to bed and a good night's sleep. The candidate should be encouraged to arise early, have a good breakfast and to arrive at the testing in plenty of time. To rush or to be late is to give away part of the advantage of his study.

The student should be coached as to testing. At the scene, no talking about the test—it will only serve to confuse; it will allow the competition to "psyche him out." When the test starts, the mechanics by now should be second nature. Careful and deliberate work, no hurry or dawdling, is the student's approach to the test. When he finishes early, he should review. When reviewing, he should not change an answer unless it is obviously incorrect—guess work at this point is destructive.

Last but not least is the essay exam, or the portion of an exam that will be essay. The trainer should instruct and test on report writing techniques and English composition techniques. He can invoke thoughts, questions and answers on today's police and social problems, and coach the candidates into the proper frame of mind.

On the day of the test, where there is an essay or essay portion of the test, the student's approach should be the same as for the multiple choice exam.

The successfully tested candidate is the reward of the training officer. It is what he is paid to produce.

Chapter 17

PREPARATION FOR ORAL EXAMINATION

To THE authors, it is axiomatic that the training officer needs to be as interested in individual officers as he is in training the various groups of officers. Consequently, the trainer should make himself available to interested candidates for promotion.

The trainer will have met these men when they received their basic training; he will have assisted them in various forms of in-service training, and he may have taught them at various of the voluntary training functions. Indeed, at this stage of the game, the trainer may be even then instructing the same individuals at the sergeants school.

The trainer has made his files available, or at least has made material from his files available to promotional candidates. The fact is that this man has made available all forms of training materials extant.

Whether the candidate has availed himself of the assistance available is, of course, up to him. Each man is free to choose his own path.

For the amenable candidates, the trainer needs to portray the backgrounds and philosophies, such as they may be, to them. He needs to show to each candidate the vagaries of the oral examination.

The oral examination is of itself an interesting and unique experience. It is the duty of the trainer to examine the full import of the test, and to delve into, with the candidate, the vagaries and problems extant therein.

The Trainer may deal with the promotional candidates individually or in a group. He should lecture, or at least verbally explain what an oral board is designed to do and how various types of board members conduct their inquisition.

Although a board will ask some "right or wrong" questions, they are primarily interested in the evaluation of personality,

The candidate must be in the proper frame of mind for his examination.

bearing and articulateness of the candidate. Failing candidates can usually attribute their lack of success to a lack of demonstrated communication ability, lack of preparation, or from a fear of the unknown.

The candidate should be trained as to the organization of his department, so that he can intelligently and knowlegeably converse on it. His formal study needs to include recent court decisions, as well as past landmark decisions. He should be familiar with the prinicples of police organization and administration.

In the early stages, the trainer can pose to the candidate the expected basic questions, such as those dealing with span of control, unity of command, loyalty, and so on.

The successful candidate will be able to give reasons for his answers, to be able to discuss and explain, and occasionally to ask a question back to the board. He may not, for example, immediately recognize a court decision by name. When such a question is posed to him, and he draws a blank, he should indicate that he does not recall the case by name, and ask for guidance as to subject matter. Often, then, he will recognize the case from his studies, and will be able to feed his knowledge back to the board.

The candidate must be in the proper frame of mind for his examination. The trainer can exhort him to this purpose. Prior to the examination the candidate must be encouraged to think of nothing but the forthcoming test. He should constantly pose to himself questions about himself and his department, and the strengths and weaknesses of both. Where he doesn't know the answer, he can easily find out.

By conversing with his wife, a candidate can prepare himself to comment on his own strengths and weaknesses. So long as the officer can hold his temper, there is no one better with whom to converse on this subject than his spouse. He may even realize a side benefit in his marriage as a result of such conversation, though we do not pose here as marriage counselors in the making of this suggestion.

Having learned what his strong and weak points are (he may be considerably surprised!) he is then better able to field such questions at the oral.

Now he should practice, to himself, how to answer questions in a positive and forceful manner. He will be before the board to sell himself, and this can be accomplished by being mentally prepared, by study, by having practiced before a board, and by couching his answers in positive phraseology and salesmanship.

The trainer, having explained, guided and supervised the foregoing steps, may now assemble his candidates for another talk (or lecture if the group is large). At this point he should review what they have done, and reiterate the reasoning applying to each step. He should again illustrate and insist that the candidate(s) continue and emphasize the "frame of mind approach," previously described.

The trainer can illustrate to the candidate some of the personalities he might expect to find on an oral board. Some of those who might be described, though not all-inclusive by any means, follow. Admittedly, several of the described characteristics may be found in one inquisitor.

The veteran police commander or supervisor: he is a mixture of the hard-nosed disciplinarian and empathetic observer of the human scene. This man will not be "conned;" he has been there before and has seen it all. He will call his shots as he sees them. He is introspective and will evaluate reasons as well as answers. He knows people and he knows policemen, and is most capable of reading between the lines and in judging what is unsaid as well as what is stated.

The "liberal": this board member will want to evaluate court decisions, civil rights problems, and the use of force. He may frame questions around police community relations problems and policies, the rights of citizens, and police brutality. Gun policy is a favorite of this type.

The educator: he will want to know what the candidate has done to prepare himself for the examination, and particularly what he has done to "improve" himself over the years. He is interested in the officer's readings, community service, degrees, college plans.

The show-off: this board member is interested in showing the candidate and the other board members what he knows. His erudite questioning will devolve upon court decisions, legislation affecting police, and such matters as the relationship between coroner and homicide investigator.

The "situation" man: what do you do when you, a new sergeant, find a patrolman sleeping on duty? What if he is a friend, is defiant, or is caught a second time? What if your officer takes a candy bar while investigating an open store door? A box of candy? A valuable wrist watch?

It is important to be able to evaluate the questioner as well as the question. The candidate should not try to answer as he feels the board would want him to answer; he should answer as honestly and knowledgeably as possible. In evaluating the questioner, the candidate is trying, not to slant his answer, but to be able to see ahead to the goal being aimed at or the trap being set by his inquisitor.

The candidate needs to be able to decide when to stick by his guns when challenged on an answer. Equally important is to be able to admit a mistake when he has obviously committed one, and to make the admission unequivocably.

In admitting a mistake, the candidate should not hem and haw about it. He can state his mistake, and await the next question. He can admit the mistake, attribute it to his misinterpretation of the question, and then answer again, in light of his most recent interpretation of the question. He should do the latter when his knowledge of the subject matter is broad enough to converse at length; otherwise he should let the mistake go and hope to regain lost ground in dealing with subsequent questions.

A baseball manager helps his owner to purchase, recruit, and trade for players. He or a scout will look over the performance of individual players, and perhaps will sign them up.

Then the manager takes the team to spring practice. There the team works into physical and mental playing condition. They work on fundamentals, shag flies, practice sliding into base, play pepper games, and on and on.

The team will then play against other teams also engaged in spring training. The manager manages and observes, pares his roster to the required number of players, and prepares his charges for the season ahead. When opening day arrives, and league play is about to commence, the manager has his first team ready to go.

The players are ready to go all the way to the pennant. They have worked themselves into shape physically, and have melded together as a team. They have trained assiduously. They are prepared to play ball.

So what do they do on the day of the game? They indulge in infield practice. They practice before the game, on the same ground upon which the contest will later occur. This team will engage in infield practice on every field prior to every game of the entire season.

Detectives and soldiers do something similar. They like to

"go over the ground" and to get a feel of that ground, the detective for his investigation, the soldier for his operation, be it for practice or for real.

The police trainer has instructed and encouraged his candidates right up to the day of the ball game, in this case the oral examination. Now he needs to arrange for infield practice.

The trainer will have his candidates perform in the same setting, in the same manner, before the same kind of tribunal as they will on the fateful day of the formal and very important oral examination.

If possible, he will arrange for the use of the actual room that will be utilized for the oral. Should this not be possible, he will arrange for a similar kind room, a conference room, perhaps. Type and arrangement of furniture may be approximated to that of the actual oral chamber.

He will now arrange to assemble an actual oral board. He will not, of course, assemble the actual board which will be sitting for the test. This would be unethical, even should he know who will be on the board. Board members, too, would be duty bound to refuse to participate in the mock oral examination.

But it is not unethical to practice; it is desirable that the practice be held. The trainer will invite several supervisory types of policemen to serve on the "board." These men can be from his own or from other departments. There should be the same number on the mock oral board as there will be on the formal board.

If three is the number to be selected, we recommend one man of long experience on boards to be present as chairman. A second man should also have at least moderate oral board experience.

The third man can be inexperienced, if he himself has been a recent successful candidate before such a board. This is helpful, for it allows him to bring in questions that are currently being asked.

This also serves as a training method to prepare for him to participate as an oral examiner himself.

The board assembles, discusses procedure, and proceeds with the examination (s) . The trainer can serve as the personnel man, or the host, and bring in each candidate, introduce him to the board, and perhaps make a few qualifying remarks about the candidate to the board.

The candidate must be treated as if this were the real thing. He will have attired himself as he will on the day of the actual oral. If uniform is the order of the day, then he should be in uniform. If plain clothes are the thing to wear in that particular department (we recommend uniform!), then he should be so attired.

The uniform should be spotless, pressed, buttoned and zipped, with all tools carried, and all acouterments clean and polished. The hat can be removed, and should be placed on the table, with clean bill and polished cap shield facing the questioners, the better to dazzle them with the reflected brilliance.

If civilian clothes are worn, the candidate should dress as for a court appearance, neatly but not in the newest and most flamboyant style. Shaves and haircuts are in order, and extremes of hair styles of any type are to be avoided.

The importance of the mock oral is that it be conducted in precisely the same manner as a formal oral would be conducted. Greeting should of course be friendly, but must not be personal, even in the event examiner and candidate are acquainted. The mock oral is valueless in the event of any horseplay or levity. It must be conducted as if it were the real thing.

Questions are asked, answered, rephrased. The candidate is attacked, queried, his answers probed, challenged, accepted or rejected. The candidate answers, parries, explains, discourses, and hopefully sells himself and his wares.

The mock oral comes to an end. The candidate is dismissed and told to wait outside. Now the mock oral board enters the second phase of its work. The candidate is graded on paper in the same fashion as will be used by the formal board. The board members make written notes as to the strengths and weaknesses as exhibited by the candidate.

In grading the candidate the board should be realistic, even tough. We recommend the candidate be downgraded as opposed to upgraded. This is not a time for a favor; a favor would be misleading to the candidate. If the mock oral is to accomplish the goal, it should be longer and more difficult than the actual oral examination.

We offer one caution, however: we have asked the board to be realistic, even harsh in grading. At this stage it would be ruinous to fail a candidate. He is there to be trained and to practice, and not to be destroyed.

The candidate who does not do well should be graded at the lowest passing grade. He can then be counseled further. No harm will be done to reexamine the poorer candidate later that same day or in another session.

The candidate is subsequently called back into the chamber of horrors. Each examiner will then comment from his notes as to the strengths and weaknesses of the performance. He might offer suggestions for improvement. Comments should be in a positive vein, and the concluding remarks should be encouraging.

At this point the trainer can sum up the performance for the benefit of the candidate. He can collect the scores and notes from the board and present them to the candidate for his reference.

Somewhere in this final training session preceding the actual oral examination, the candidate should be encouraged to avoid fruitless conversations and worryings with his fellow applicants. These are mostly counterproductive in terms of gathering incorrect information from others. Not the least of the evils in this area is that of being "psyched out" by a rival. Good advice to the candidate: Let the other guy worry about you, don't you worry about him.

The trainer's job is now largely finished. The candidate now has to do the thing himself. The trainer should suggest the candidate get a good night's sleep before the big day. Intensive study on that night is to be discouraged. The candidate should plan to arise in time to breakfast, prepare and travel to his examination in a leisurely fashion.

He may not be particularly hungry on that morning, but he also does not really need a growling stomach when confronting the oral board. Likewise, he who arrives late, or he who needs to rush to arrive on time will cause unnecessary worry and distress for himself. The leisurely preparation and travel will better serve the frame of mind necessary to a good performance before the oral board.

"Congratulations, Sergeant."

The candidates reward comes in the form of blue and white chevrons. The trainer's reward comes when he can say: "Congratulations, Sergeant."

Chapter 18

INSTRUCTING POLICE SUPERVISORS

Sᴇʀɢᴇᴀɴᴛs, lieutenants and captains are a particularly difficult group to instruct on almost any subject. These are people who handle people of all types all of the time. They handle policemen and they handle the public. They are charged with handling the matter when the citizen and the officer are at odds as to fact, policy, demeanor, or approach.

They are policemen and they are supervisors of policemen. Some of them supervise other police supervisors. Many of them are, and all of them should be instructors in their own right. They are suspicious people and they are largely paranoid. The former is necessarily acquired to survive in the calling; the latter is an occupationally caused disease.

A group of supervisors, summoned to an in-service training class, will arrive at that place, but are likely to be somewhat intransigent. The attitude is likely to be one of "Show me; I don't believe you can show me. Who the hell are you? That's not the way we do it on the street. What are *they* (police administration) going to do to us now?"

Supervisors attending college classes for their own improvement, or perhaps because the department has an educational pay incentive increment, are somewhat the same. They tend to set their own examples for the class, to prove or disprove the point made by the instructor. They tend to "expert" the instructor. This is normally accomplished in a diplomatic fashion, but it is done, nonetheless.

Thus do police supervisors keep an instructor "honest"; very, very honest. And so does the instructor, of whatever rank, face his challenge: how to instruct supervisors.

The instructor, again, of whatever rank, should proceed with diplomacy, modesty in his own achievements, praise for the achievements of the "students."

"Okay, boys, be alert!"

He should readily acknowledge the expertise of his charges. Through tact, persuasiveness and judiciously applied praise, develop the group into students—and at the same time he should draw upon those students as source persons.

"Captain, tomorrow the class will discuss crowd handling. You were in command during that riot at the Cow Palace. Would you mind filling us in on the problems you faced on that day?"

The captain will be delighted to do just that. The instructor's problem will be to retain control of his class, lest the captain take it over. By applied conference leading techniques, however, the instructor can extract the fact (and fantasy) material from the captain, and still get the points of the lesson across to the class.

The captain and his men will have made mistakes at the riot. These can be discussed without demeaning anyone; a frank acknowledgement and discussion of mistakes is necessary to the lesson. These should be sandwiched between what was done right, such as quick response to the scene and excellent court identification of those arrested.

Others of the group will explain away the captain's mistakes. The instructor should allow this to a point. In this fashion, he will encourage and enlist the support of the friends of the captain. Others will be somewhat critical—they may be either critical friends of the man or they may be his administrative enemies. They should be encouraged to comment, not insultingly, and thus will they be won over to the spirit of the classroom.

Participation by the students, just accomplished, gets the show on the road. All hands feel they are members of the group. However unwillingly at first, they will get the group feeling; most will participate, toward the end very willingly.

The instructor should tell the group why they are there, and what they are going to do and why. He will deliver a short lecture before the discussion, and will sum up after. In between, subject matter permitting, he should utilize the discussion method of instruction.

Discussion is well suited to police supervisors. They are problem solvers, and are extremely adaptable to team effort and to role playing; after all these are their stock in trade—theirs is a team effort and they do role play nightly.

Such a group has all sorts of experience in it. By assigning problems to the students, the instructor will elicit a usually willing response. Heretofore unsuspected solutions will be forthcoming to a given problem. Should a solution be patiently unworkable, the group itself will let the fellow student know in their critique. The instructor should always take care to praise his student for his work and for his novel solution, even should the group feel it to be unworkable.

Sensitivity training, the "classroom in the round" is valuable for such a group. Administrative matters, personnel policies, intradepartmental hangups may well be resolved in such a fashion.

The trick is to convince the students to speak up at any time during the class, to verbally attack each other as necessary, and to pound out solutions to problems in this fashion.

Such training sessions should be four or five hours in length; at the end should always be a cooling off period, so that an argument does not go back to the job with the policemen. It helps to break bread, to lunch together at the end of and as part of the class session.

The lowest ranking men present will be the most reluctant to stick their necks out in give and take discussion. The instructor can encourage this by getting the ranking men going, even by employing a preinstructed stooge or two at a particular session.

Outside experts are most helpful in this type of class. Newsmen, Black Panthers, social workers, educators, are good choices. They should be instructed to expound on their own backgrounds, hangups, and to praise where possible and to fault the police where that applies. The instructor should employ his negative expert at the end of the course. Those officers who jousted in earlier sessions are noticably pulled back together by a "threat" from the "outside."

Such instruction is most valuable when students from several departments are present. If properly handled, when the last class is finished, the students for the most part have a bond between them that did not exist before. Having participated together in the give and take of the classes, they have something more in common than heretofore, to be referred to, sometimes laughingly, at future meetings on the job.

The instructor should take great care to properly credit his students, to get them to participate, and to draw upon their expertise. The accumulated experience of such a group is truly staggering.

The type of instruction is up to the instructor in most cases. Utilizing any and all techniques discussed in this book, the instructor should find such a group responding best to discussion and sensitivity class approaches.

At times it will be unrealistic to mix the ranks in a sensitivity type of class. We say it can and does work extremely well, very profitably, and we speak from experience. Where the climate of the department, department politics, or whatever, would preclude the judicious instructor from employing the method, he can still do so in modified form.

The answer is simple and workable. Do not mix the ranks. Approach the ranks one at a time. Thus: a sergeant's class, lieutenants' class, and so on. When there are an insufficient number of a given rank in a department to profitably hold a class, then a mix of several departments, one rank, is the answer. It works.

Chapter 19

DISCIPLINE AND PERSONNEL
INVESTIGATIONS

EVERYTHING in training should tend to encourage and establish positive discipline. Positive discipline, for our purposes, will be defined here as a "voluntary and eager conformance with existing on-going high standards of the department and the profession."

Discipline is best instilled at the recruit level. The training officer and his staff are in the unique position of "bending the twig." As discussed in the chapter on the "police academy," a difficult period of stress training, coupled with an overemphasis on all forms of physical training, inspections, rank courtesies, and some rote training is where discipline begins. Strong and positive line supervision will nurture the bent twig into a sturdy police oak tree.

Training for discipline, then, of necessity includes the line supervisors. As we state elsewhere in this book, to train a new policeman and then to throw him to the wolves, in this case disgruntled or ignorant line supervisors, is to waste everyone's time and effort. The supervisors need training in the same matters, though often from a somewhat different point of view.

Positive discipline will cause a man to function in the prescribed manner when he is tired, wet, hungry, frightened and/or generally unhappy. Discipline, then must be instilled, ingrained, nurtured. Morale is to discipline as mother's milk is to the infant.

For some reason, when "morale" is mentioned in police work, the word contains a negative implication. Often, to say morale, the police jargon really means "bad morale." Policemen almost never say "good morale." They are more likely to say "He feels good," "Things are going OK," "The boys are doing a good job."

Although it goes unverbalized, we feel that policemen have in general equated "morale" with "bad" and "esprit d'corps" with good morale. This is really a commentary of the negativism of police work, so much so that it has become part of the anomie of the policeman.

We wish to emphasize here that "morale" can and should be both good and positive, as discipline can be good and positive. This should run through the entire organization. The trainer, and his crew, will bend the twig, or plant the seed, or whatever. Good, positive, hard, fair discipline by the leaders, the supervisors, will nurture that morale. The trainer has a role here, also, for it will be he who will keep those leaders going through inservice, sergeant school, and/or bulletin training.

Morale "filters down from the top, it does not bubble up from the bottom." It will help, then, that the trainer and/or supervisors he has trained, will climb to departmental policy level positions over the long haul. The Chief of Police and his immediate subordinate supervisors are the ones who start the filtering process.

Thus far, then, we have spoken herein of positive matters vis a vis discipline and morale. When negative discipline must be invoked (suspension, reprimand, dismissal), then "discipline" has actually failed. Punishment will extract the pound of flesh from the malefactor, and does serve as an example to the other officers; but, essentially, the need to apply negative discipline points up the failure of discipline.

Policemen being men, and men being what they are, negative discipline is inevitable in any organization. The only real indication of good or bad morale or good or bad discipline is the frequency of the sinning.

The very writing and very content and subject matter of this book is essentially positive in nature. Good discipline and strong morale are touched upon throughout, directly or indirectly. The remainder of this chapter will deal with a negative. We will talk of how to investigate personnel, how to build a personnel case, and how to instruct the police leader in these unhappy, unwanted, necessary tasks.

It is the task of the training officer to instruct the supervisors as to both the necessity and the method of personnel investigation. He does this by example, lecture, demonstration. He will instill into the student the necessity for being able to properly so investigate. The key point to sell and resell is that a personnel matter is not difficult to investigate, it is merely unpalatable to the average investigator. It is, however, one of the things that a supervisor is paid to do; if he cannot stand the heat, he should get out of the kitchen.

Are you helping anyone?

A specific complaint against or identified problem with personnel should be investigated, immediately and assiduously. Such a matter should be approached in the same fashion as one would investigate a criminal matter. Obviously, a personnel matter can be criminal, administrative, or some combination in nature. Evidence, statements, reports and exhibits are to be handled just as though, in each instance, the matter is going to result in a hearing. Said hearing can be in court, can be quasi-judicial (as with a personnel board), or both.

The investigator in each instance should try to establish guilt or innocence. He should work as hard to clear an innocent man as he should to convict a guilty one. In either case, the investigator should establish a hard and clear case.

He needs to have a complete case, for example, to convict his man at a hearing. He should have a clear and established case to prove innocence; this latter is both for the good of the personnel and to obviate possible future "whitewashing" charges against the investigator and the department.

It is important for the department to win personnel cases that go to hearing. It is essential for overall discipline. To lose too many cases is to dilute discipline.

However, ineluctably, some cases will be lost at the personnel board level. This will occur because of an improperly prepared case, or because the board is particularly sympathetic to personnel, or as the result of the board's liberal "live and let live, give the benefit of all doubt" philosophy.

Having lost, when this occurs, the department should be prepared to proceed again. When the renegade officer gets in trouble again, the same approach should be employed by the department. It should be clear to all that the department, in the interest of discipline and justice, is prepared to go all the way on each case, for as many times as it takes. Eventually, the recalcitrant officer will either get the idea, and reform, or he will get tired of the expense of attorneys time after time, or he will, logically and correctly, be separated from the service.

To repeat: this is not to imply that all accused personnel are guilty, by any means. A strong case should be made for the innocent man, without question.

There are two schools of thought relative to the investigator of personnel. One school holds that this person should be a gatherer of fact, should present facts gathered, and that further decision and action is to be implemented at an administrative level.

The other school holds that the investigator should accompany his report with recommendation for type of action, if any, to be taken.

The argument in favor of the first option is one of objectivity. In the second case, the investigator's recommendation is still only that, a recommendation. Report review and implementation of action still rests with the higher level.

The authors do not opt for either school of thought. What works best for a given department is what is best for that department. Departmental policy prevails in any event. Our departmental policy (Daly City, California) calls for the recommendation to be made by the investigator. This works successfully in this particular department.

The true personnel case starts before the man is appointed to the department. It consists of early and continuous documentation. While admittedly this is somewhat subject to policy, such documentation can be accomplished without opposing an administration that does not have a stated or ongoing policy of this type.

Assume that, at the applicant level, the department conducts an oral board at which potential policemen are questioned. At the board should be a member of the department. This man may or may not be an official board member, and he may or may not be allowed to ask questions. If at all legally possible, however, a departmental representative should be present.

In addition to the usual questions and elicitation of information from the applicant, other matters should be established. If the departmental representative is not allowed to speak, he should cause his questions to be asked by others.

A line of questioning follows. It is not all-inclusive, but should serve to establish what is necessary:

1. Do you realize the necessity for following orders?
2. Are you prepared to follow the orders and directions of your sergeant?

3. You will not always agree with your sergeant. Are you still prepared to follow his direction? (Examples can be discussed here.)

4. You will be required, if appointed, to adhere to haircut and uniform regulations. Your shoes must be shined, for example. Are you prepared to do this? Are you sure?

5. You will occasionally have an opportunity to discuss departmental policies and procedures. However, those policies and procedures in force will prevail. Are you prepared to follow them? Are you sure?

6. These questions and answers will be documented. If you are appointed to the department, the documentation will be inserted into your personnel file. Do you understand?

7. In event of future misunderstanding or problem, I or another supervisor may someday remind you of our conversation of today. Is this clear? Do you understand?

Should anything not be clear to the candidate, of course it should be made clear. Understanding is paramount.

Following the oral board, the departmental representative will reduce to writing his findings. He will create a memorandum indicating the names of the candidates present for examination, as well as the names of the inquisitors (these latter for future witnesses as may be necessary). He will then include the questions, as listed above, and indicate understanding and acquiescence on the part of the candidate. He should then cause the appropriate routings of the memorandum. Each successful candidate should have one in his file. This is the first piece of paper, so important, in the future, potential personnel case.

Later, and as necessary the promise should be made good. When the officer feuds with his sergeant, when he refuses to have his hair trimmed, when he negatively and maliciously attacks departmental policy, the above described memo should be shown him. Usually, it will slow down the malcontent, and will even restore a sense of perspective to the misguided or temporarily disaffected officer. Remind him of his promises.

Remind him of his promises, and record and verify the reminder. Write it down. Tell him you are writing it down. Give him a copy. Have him sign for his copy. Have a witness. List the witness. Document everything.

During Police Academy training, of course, said training is documented in all phases. Instructor names, names of the entire class, dates and times, all are recorded. This, to later show that the man *was* in fact properly and appropriately trained in, say, gun policy. Thus, when he shoots the jaywalking pedestrian, he cannot claim ignorance or noninstruction. That part of the case is made, in the unhappy event it becomes necessary to make it.

All transfers, voluntary extra duty, admonishments, commendations, all, everything, is documented and filed. It all goes to make the eventual personnel case for or against the man in the long run. It will tend to help him in establishing a continuing code of conduct. Save for the individual flagrant violation (rape, arson, drunkenness), oftentimes accusations have to do with an officer's mannerisms, general ability and demeanor, thoroughness, the like. A long-standing continuing record can well serve to refute such charges.

Evaluations go into the records. This is not a chapter on evaluations. However, evaluations assist in making the personnel case. To this extent we speak here of evaluations. The report card, with comments, or a copy thereof, belongs here. Positive statements are included. Where and when there are deficiencies in appearance or work performance, these are noted. *In each instance, there should be stated what corrective action was attempted by the supervisor and what the results are to date!* It is essential to show the corrective action—to merely list deficiencies does not show leadership and training, and can harm the potential personnel case. Hopefully, such instruction will obviate the necessity for that case!

There will develop in any department the renegade officer, the one who goes bad. In terms of investigation and prosecution, dismissal or whatever, the individual flagrant violation is the easiest to handle. More difficult is the borderline defiance and rule breaking problem. Complete and continuing documentation of the problems extant is the answer.

The trainer, again, must continue to train the supervisor to write it down, get it witnessed, tell the man it is being written and filed, give him a copy, have him sign for the copy, include corrective action on the memorandum. This *is* the personnel case when the time comes to pursue it.

A personnel investigation differs from a criminal investigation only in matter of degree. It is easier than is the criminal investigation in that witnesses and documentation are more readily obtainable. Other policemen, people who reside on the beats, city and other officials, are available for interview. Records, police reports or personnel records and the like, rarely disappear. They are available for perusal.

The personnel investigation is more difficult, usually, than the criminal investigation in another area. The city official will complain about an officer's conduct, but will not witness against him. Citizens will complain out of spite or for an exacting of revenge against the policeman, or more realistically, against the body of police. Lastly and understandably, policemen usually do not want to inform or witness against brother officers. To be sure, policemen are gossips, for it is in the very nature of their work; but they do not like to officially injure the brother officer.

The reasons for this latter attitude are many. The officers work together; they feel somewhat oppressed by the media and the public; they do not want to throw another man to the wolves; last but not least, in the brotherhood runs the feeling, spoken or not, that "there but for the grace of God go I."

So, witnesses are usually easier to find, and somewhat more difficult to make talk in the police personnel case as opposed to the criminal case. All in all, however, the personnel case is in the long run simpler to make than is the criminal matter. The competent, sincere investigator just has much more going for him in the personnel matter.

For the trainer, instruction of supervisors to this end is a difficult task indeed. They will verbally and personally defend "the men." This is fine, and we hope and trust that they really do feel this way about the men. That feeling can be channeled into their training and supervisory efforts; if a man rates a commendation, get him one; if he needs help, give it to him, and the like.

Some supervisors will espouse empathy and compassion for "the men," and they lie. What they are really saying is "I don't want the unpopular and difficult task of taking on a policeman." This type of supervisor wouldn't lift a finger to help "the men," such as aiding in difficult cases, extra instruction, an understanding and available ear for the man's problems. He is being selfish. He is thinking of himself, not "the men," and last of all the department.

The trainer should endeavor to reach those supervisors who really do help their men. More of the same help might prevent some personnel matters from occurring. However, the salient point to espouse and nail down is that it doesn't help a man to allow him to get away with flagrant violations or with a continuing code of conduct injurious to the public, to the department, and to himself.

The man should be corrected. It is a matter of supervision. The flagrant matter, or the continuing smaller problem, must be investigated. The supervisor is not helping the man if he does nothing about it. After all, who is who's friend? The sergeant should assist his man, but the man who continually through his action or lack of it puts the sergeant on the spot, is he truly a friend of the sergeant? He is not; he is a spoiled boy, expecting favors throughout life.

The trainer should instruct supervisors in class, and carefully and completely. Departmental policies need to be clear. This includes not only written policies. To go on the policy only as written is insanity. The trainer here needs the understanding and backing of the powers that be. *Then* he can discuss policy with the sergeants and lieutenants.

Tape recordings and other evidence of personnel matters should be used. A tape recording, for example, is "living proof" of the matter being discussed. Case reports are helpful, also, if the trainer can get these released for school purposes.

Obviously, no case still pending hearing or awaiting appeal should be used in the class. Also, a saving statement is essential. The trainer must make clear that he is endeavoring to embarrass or demean no one. It is a professional police class, he should say, it is a closed class, and what is said there stays there. He is interested in conveying knowledge of policy and procedure in personnel matters. The statement should be documented, in the not unlikely event that a sergeant will confront a person who has been investigated with embarrassing statements or questions. That sergeant should be taken to task administratively.

The mission of the trainer here is to focus upon and develop the necessary skills of the supervisor. The development of frame of mind is an integral part of the approach and the goal. Definitely, the trainer does not want to develop a "headhunting" supervisor. Sadism and cruelty in this area are reprehensible and not to be tolerated.

The supervisor who learns to enjoy conducting personnel investigations is not a leader; he is a detriment to the department, the morale, the personnel. That supervisor needs counseling, retraining, and in some cases, negative discipline employed upon him.

Chapter 20

ADMINISTRATIVE TRAINING

ADMINISTRATIVE TRAINING has been among the most neglected of training programs. How true the saying: "Too often the Chief of Police is not an administrator; he is merely a 'promoted police-men'!"

This statement, possibly apocryphal, is a generalization. The statement is easily applicable to the Chief's administrative personnel. It is applicable all too often to the Chief, his deputy chiefs, captains, often to the lieutenants (depending upon type of assignment), as well as to many of the special appointees (including training officers!).

Because the "promoted policeman" holds an exalted rank, because he has become a "prince of the department," does not mean that he knows what he is doing. It means that he has served well in his previous rank, that he is an accomplished test taker, and that he has been rewarded via promotion. The authors do not say there is anything wrong with these things—for after all, the authors are among that group being written about.

We do say that such promotees, old hands and young ones, are not usually sufficiently prepared for their new responsibilities. For example, because a man is a deputy chief, a seasoned veteran and a man of commanding presence, does not imply that he is the man to decide upon purchase of equipment and implementation of training for a new video tape closed circuit television program. Because he is a commander doesn't mean he is an expert in all things. He is *not* an expert in all things. Far, far from it.

Some policemen complain, rightly so, about elected officials. The complaint goes something like this: "You take a man off the street. He has good presence and can talk. Someone backs him with money and influence. Now he is a city councilman. And now, suddenly, miraculously, this man is an expert on water matters, he second guesses the engineer, is an honorary fire chief, and other things. First and foremost, and everlastingly, he is a law enforcement expert. He is the local supreme court, ombudsman, and civilian review board all in one."

That not too exaggerated example is applicable to the police commander. Because he knows people, is a leader, and has been "around the block" a few times, does not mean he is a trainer, or a businessman, or an equipment expert. The solution? He should learn these subjects, or he should surround himself with bright young policemen who do know these things. The answer is simple, once we cut through the lethargy and suspicion of that commander and once we get the Chief to cut loose with some training funds.

Obviously, we need to convince that commander that it is not a sign of weakness not to know everything, and that it is not a sign of weakness to take a class or two. Getting the money from the Chief of Police is another matter, indeed.

In hiring, we should pay as much attention to obtaining the college business major as we do to the police science major. Failing this, and in addition to it, we should endeavour to send selected officers to school to major in business, as well as other courses of study. This is not to neglect police science per se, but is meant to round out police personnel backgrounds and qualifications.

Certainly, the administrator and his staff should not be neglected in this type of training. Area schools should be taken advantage of. Admittedly, this gets into the policy area; the trainer needs to "make his case" to the Chief, complete with arguments in favor of such schooling, as well as the ramifications of the entire program.

California has the Peace Officers Standards and Training Program. The P.O.S.T. program is state subsidized; even salaries are reimbursable to the jurisdiction sending students. The program includes all levels and phases from recruit basic academy through the executive himself, in this case the Chief of Police.

There are middle management schools, and there are upper management schools and seminars. The only cost to the department is the absence of the student from his normal duties; the compensation is the attained knowledge of that student. He should be able to return to his duties more qualified in peripheral areas than heretofore; he should be required to share his knowledge, newly gained, as applicable.

In the medium-sized department, the argument is "How can we afford to send a captain away for two weeks, and which of my three captains should I send?"

The answer is relatively simple. We cannot afford *not* to send a captain. Better to send all three, sequentially or at one time.

What? Send all three captains simultaneously? Certainly. Vacations and sick time will sometimes cause the absence of these worthies. They all have understudies. Turn over duties to their assistants. Make it a test program for these subordinates. Let us prove whether they can, in fact, function when they must take over in emergency.

In this fashion, we have two on-going training programs. The assistants function in the next higher capacity, and the bosses improve administratively. By sending, in this case, all three captains, the training is not dragged out, but is completed in the shortest possible time. Of course, where and when the department must provide funds for such schools (not so in the case of P.O.S.T.), then the administrative training might need to be spread over a period of time. In either event, "can't afford the man or the money" is an illogical and counterproductive excuse on the part of administration. The farsighted and progressive administrator will find a way to do it. We have suggested a way above.

Administrative training might also be carried out in-house. Here the trainer might set up lesson plans and seminars. The trainer, an outside expert, or an invited outside administrative type(s) can be invited to lecture, explain, or to conduct exercises. Said exercises can be of the command-post type, wherein problems and conditions can be simulated, hopefully to be solved on the spot by the local commanders and staff people.

The United States Army was one of the earliest organizations to productively use staff and to develop staff functions. Assistance can be obtained from this source. Some of the large corporations, perhaps utility companies, are happy to assist in such training, and are more than capable of providing staff and know-how to this end.

*Peace Officers Standards and Training.

With respect to teaching and learning existing and on-going staff procedures, we recommend a form of on-the-job training. One method of accomplishing this is to establish a rotating administrative assistant slot. A new Lieutenant probably knows his street work and the overall organization, by virtue of his intelligence, past training, and recent experiences as sergeant. How now to introduce him to and into the management team?

Again, the trainer needs to sell the administrator on the program. Having done this, the trainer devises the program and implements it. He will oversee the program from a guiding and critical standpoint. He will need to convince the student (lieutenant in this case), and the unit supervisors as to the efficacy of the program.

Once this is accomplished, the program is ready to be started. The lieutenant is relieved from his line duties and is temporarily assigned to a rotating administrative training program.

The lieutenant should then work for one week in each of detectives, Training, Uniform Commander's Office, Records, any other unit extant, and the office of the Chief of Police. At these locations, the lieutenant understudies the commander, works personnel matters, assignment matters, and fields the ineluctable and sequential daily crises peculiar to that post.

The theory of the assignments is to give insight into the administrative problems extant and inherent in each unit. The assignee would be allowed to understudy the commander; he should be allowed to work at tasks that match his instruction and knowledge; he should not be given "busy" work. At the conclusion of his tour of duty with each unit, the lieutenant should be required to prepare a report of his experiences and understandings, including comments and criticisms. His fresh and objective insight might allow for suggestions that would simplify some of the tasks, even though this is not a primary goal of such an assignment.

This is both administrative training and an indoctrination period. It allows administrative personnel to work with someone fresh from the street, and hopefully will make street problems more real to these personnel. At best, too, the new lieutenant will have become a member of the management team.

The graduate. Is he also trained?

Administrative training can be further enhanced by cross-training with other departments. By mutual agreement, two police departments can profitably exchange counterparts, be they lieutenants or assistant chiefs, for a period of time. The training can be carried out in a manner similar to that described for the lieutenant in the rotating slot. This has been done between large departments from different countries; surely it will be valuable at the local levels. All of the arguments apply.

Policy is one of the hangups in this type of training. The training officer may have a job in selling the Chief of Police as to the validity and efficacy of administrative training. The trainer is obligated to do his homework and to sell the concept. Should the department have a form of administrative training, then it is the task of the trainer to sell an expansion of that program. Once it is sold, then the trainer will oversee and babysit the program(s) and properly document same.

Chapter 21

TRAINING FILES AND LESSON PLANS

We have mentioned in this book that the training officer should maintain an up-to-date training file. This file should contain all lesson plans submitted by his instructors, as well as all pertinent writings that relate to the material.

The file should be kept under the control of the training officer, and it should be available only under his direct supervision. It is foolish to leave the files where they are accessible to the general staff. Officers will extract lessons or publications to study for an examination, or just to improve their knowledge. Unfortunately, they often fail to return the material, and it is lost to the training division forever.

In order for the training file to be complete and worthwhile, it should include motion pictures, video tapes, tape recordings and the like, in addition to the written word.

The file must be up-to-date. Training bulletins that apply to court decisions that have been overruled should be discarded, or at least taken from the active file. Material that is out-of-date is of little value in the file and it still takes space.

We suggest a card control file for the material, cross-indexed by alphabetical listing and then by a code numbering system, by category. For example, we might list: Robbery, Lesson plan for in-progress response 15-1.

This would indicate the general category, Robbery, the specific material covered in the lesson plan, and the section of the file where it might be found, Section 15, Item #1.

In this manner, as new material is added to a general section, it is simply added as another item under the main heading. If the item is stored in some place other than the filing cabinet, the card should designate the place of storage.

We also suggest that items of equipment assigned to the division should also be inventoried and a control kept on their use and storage.

A complete, up-to-date training file is one of the most important tools available to the training officer.

What follows in this chapter is a collection of sample lesson plans taken from the files of the Daly City Police Department. Some of the plans are lengthy and obviously require long, involved classes to teach. Some are short and are designed to be delivered in one or two brief sessions at roll call. In each case, the title is clearly stated and the material spelled out so that experienced police instructor could teach the lesson with little prior preparation.

We offer these as examples with the hope that they will be of some value to the reader, from the point of view of format, if not for specific information content.

CITY OF DALY CITY INTER-OFFICE MEMORANDUM

TO: TRAINING DIVISION   DATE 7-1-71
FROM: STAFF BUREAU
SUBJECT: DISTRIBUTION OF TRAINING BULLETINS

1. Training Bulletins are normally submitted to Chief's Office for approval prior to distribution. This is particularly true and important when the policy, procedure, and attitude are involved. In all cases Training Bulletins will be approved by Staff Bureau Manager prior to submission to the Chief. And, in instances where the material originates with a member other than the writer of the Training Bulletin, this other member should be given the opportunity to approve of its contents or disclaim authorship prior to submission.

2. Routing: Chief (1); Bureaus (3) (ACOP; C/HANSEN; C/ SIMS); Det. Div.; Training (2) (original and one copy); POST (Training Folder); and, additionally, specifically involved members, i.e. Lab. Tech., Range Master, etc., if the subject matter is their specialty, or if they are to instruct or administer to a change, etc.; and, additionally, if approved by Staff

Mgr., for additional distribution, i.e. *Capt. HANSEN receives one additional copy of all Bulletins.* TEN (10) COPIES WILL ACCOMMODATE THE ABOVE DISTRIBUTION.

3. This note will be reduced to and be included in a Training Bulletin on Training Bulletin Format, Structure, Production, and Routing.

S.F.STEEN #23, Staff Bureau
7-1-71

TRAINING  DIVISION

We run a  "taught" ship.

STUDY MATERIAL

SPELLING

This is a list of 303 words used in police reports that are often misspelled.

In terms of accuracy, it is very important that the reporting police officer be able to properly spell the words.

Most of these words are frequently used in police reports; *All* of these words are occasionally used in police reports.

1. abandon	20. anonymous	39. burglary
2. abrasion	21. answered	40. business
3. accepted	22. apparently	41. cafeteria
4. access	23. appearance	42. caliber
5. accessible	24. argumentative	43. carburetor
6. accidentally	25. articles	44. ceiling
7. acquired	26. assistance	45. characteristic
8. address	27. attached	46. chose
9. admission	28. attempted	47. cigarette
10. admitted	29. attendant	48. commenced
11. advice	30. acknowledged	49. commission
12. advised	31. assumed	50. commit
13. aggravated	32. barbiturate	51. committing
14. alcohol	33. believed	52. committed
15. alleged	34. beverage	53. comparison
16. altercation	35. bicycle	54. compelled
17. altered	36. boisterous	55. complained
18. analysis	37. bruised	56. concealed
19. analyzed	38. bureau	57. consistent

159

58. contusion	103. fictitious	148. judgment
59. cooperative	104. fight	149. judgement
60. coroner	105. forcible	150. juvenile
61. counsel	106. foreign	151. khaki
62. cursory	107. freight	152. kidnaped
63. damaged	108. frightened	153. kidnapped
64. debt	109. frequency	154. knowledge
65. deceased	110. garage	155. knuckles
66. deceived	111. gauge	156. laboratory
67. decision	112. gradually	157. laceration
68. defecated	113. guarantee	158. language
69. defendant	114. guided	159. latent
70. definite	115. guilty	160. lawyer
71. delinquent	116. habitually	161. legitimate
72. dependent	117. handkerchief	162. length
73. deployed	118. heard	163. loitering
74. described	119. height	164. legible
75. destination	120. hemorrhage	165. lieutenant
76. developed	121. heroin	166. lewd
77. diagnosis	122. hindered	167. liable
78. diesel	123. homicide	168. license
79. disappearance	124. horizontal	169. liquid
80. disclosed	125. hurriedly	170. liquor
81. disguise	126. hysterical	171. location
82. dispute	127. illiterate	172. loose
83. distinguishing	128. imagined	173. magazine
84. disturbance	129. inadequately	174. maintained
85. drunken	130. interceded	175. maintenance
86. dual	131. irrelevant	176. malicious
87. eighth	132. intoxicated	177. maneuvered
88. eligible	133. indicating	178. manufacturing
89. embarrassed	134. involuntary	179. marijuana
90. employee	135. immediately	180. marihuana
91. entrance	136. incidentally	181. masturbating
92. epileptic	137. independent	182. meant
93. equipment	138. inhabitant	183. meaning
94. evidence	139. innocence	184. medicine
95. exaggerated	140. instead	185. medication
96. examined	141. insufficent	186. memorandum
97. exceeded	142. insured	187. mileage
98. excessive	143. interior	188. minimum
99. extremely	144. interrupted	189. miscellaneous
100. facility	145. investigation	190. moisture
101 familiar	146. jealous	191. multiple
102. fatal	147. jeopardize	192. municipal

193. murdered
194. mustache
195. narcotics
196. noticeable
197. nuisance
198. necessary
199. neighborhood
200. notification
201. numerous
202. occurs
203. occurring
204. occurrence
205. omitted
206. obscene
207. occasion
208. occasionally
209. occupation
210. offense
211. opportunity
212. organized
213. original
214. overt
215. parallel
216. parole
217. probation
218. partial
219. participated
220. particularly
221. peculiar
222. pedestrian
223. penis
224. performance
225. perishable
226. permissible
227. persistent
228. personnel
229. persuaded

230. physical
231. possession
232. possibly
233. preceded
234. preference
235. pregnant
236. prepared
237. prescription
238. presence
239. prevalent
240. previously
241. pried
242. principal
243. prisoner
244. privilege
245. probable
246. proceeded
247. procedure
248. psychologist
249. pursuit
250. pursued
251. quarrel
252. quantity
253. realized
254. receipt
255. recipient
256. recognized
257. referred
258. registered
259. released
260. relevant
261. residence
262. resisted
263. resistance
264. repeated
265. restrained
266. scene

267. scissors
268. secretary
269. sedative
270. seizure
271. separate
272. sergeant
273. severed
274. severely
275. sheriff
276. shoulder
277. signature
278. significant
279. similar
280. shimmed
281. specific
282. specimen
283. stationary
284. stomach
285. straight
286. subdued
287. succeed
288. sufficient
289. suicide
290. suite
291. suspect
292. tenant
293. thorough
294. through
295. typical
296. unconscious
297. vertical
298. victim
299. violation
300. visible
301. witnessed
302. writing
303. yielded

CHEMICAL AGENT TRAINING COURSE

North San Mateo County Police Department Personnel

Conducted May – June, 1970

at

Classroom lecture and videotape recording at

DALY CITY POLICE DEPARTMENT

Range and Field Demonstration and Participation at

PACIFICA POLICE RANGE

Coordinated by: Robert La Berge, Sergeant
Training Division—Redwood City Police
Department

Staff:	David L. Bratton	Lieutenant	California State Police
	Ray Savage	Chief of Police	Broadmoor Police Department
	Al Lagomarsino	Chief of Police	Colma Police Department
	James Swinford	Sergeant	So. S.F. Police Department
	Al Tebaldi	Captain	Pacifica Police Department
	William Cann	Captain	San Bruno Police Department
	David Hansen	Captain	Daly City Police Department
	Robert Ingbrigtsen	Sergeant	Daly City Police Department

CHEMICAL AGENT TRAINING COURSE

I. HISTORICAL, MEDICAL AND LEGAL ASPECTS

A. INTRODUCTION, ORIENTATION AND OVER-
VIEW

1.   was passed with the inten-
tion of bringing knowledge of this subject to members of all law enforcement agencies.

We want to emphasize one point:

2. HISTORY AND PHILOSOPHY
   a. TEAR GAS DEFINED

II. TYPES OF NONLETHAL CHEMICAL AGENTS
   A. TYPES OF TEAR GAS
      1. CN (Chloroacetophenone—"Cry Now")
      2. CS (Orthochlorbenzalmalono Nitrile — "Chicken Shit")
      3. DM (Diphenylamine Chloroarsine or Adamsite)
      4. HC (Smoke)
   B.
   C. The primary purpose for using tear smoke is to reduce a
   _____.
   It is best used where gas can be sent into an area whereby it would_____.
   The basic rule is to_____.

III.

IV. MEDICAL REPORTS
   A. PHYSIOLOGICAL AND PSYCHOLOGICAL EFFECTS
      1. CN
      2. CS
      3. DM
      4. MACE

V. TEAR GAS LAWS
   A. WHO MAY POSSESS
      Penal Code Sections_____, explicitly, Section _____which gives us the first authority to use gas.
   B. UNDER WHAT CONDITIONS
      Determined by_____and by_____
      _____.
   C. SECURITY AND CONTROL
      1. Sale is now strictly controlled by law.
      2. Beginning_____, the State Public Health Service must approve all gas munitions used in the State.

VI.

VII. EXAMINATION
    A. TACTICAL EMPLOYMENT (Theory)
       1. IDENTIFICATION
          a. *SIGHT*
            1)
            2)
            3)
            4)
       2. How to identify container contents by:
          a. *SIGHT*
            1)
            2)

    B. OPERATION—HOW THEY WORK
       1. Mechanical and chemical components and safety:
          a. GRENADE TYPES
            1) The arming lever is called the_____.
            2) The fuse, arming pin, fuse adaptor combination is called the_____.
            3)
            4)
            5)

VIII. EXAMINATION
    A. BASEBALL TYPES
       1.
       2.
       3.

    B. CARTRIDGES
       1.
       2.
       3.

    C. FOUR TYPES OF DELIVERY SYSTEMS
       1.
          a.
          b.

c.

d.

e.

f. Tactical uses are:

  1)

  2)

2. BURN OR PYROTECHNIC
  a. ADVANTAGES:

  b. DISADVANTAGES:

  c. TACTICAL USE:

3. FOG
  a. ADVANTAGES:

  b. DISADVANTAGES:

  c. TACTICAL USE:

4. DISPENSERS USED
  a. GRENADES

  b. PROJECTILES AND CARTRIDGES

    1) How to deliver

      a)

      b)

      c)

      d)

      e)

      f)

  c. GAS GUN

    1) Description

    2) Use

    3) Safety factor

    4) Care and cleaning

  d. GRENADE LAUNCHERS

    1) Description

      a) Shotgun

      b) Pistol

      c) 37mm

e. IRRITANT DISPERSERS
  1) Use
  2) Safety factors
  3) Care

f. CHEMICAL SPRAYS
  1) Types
  2) Dispensers
  3) Use

g. IRRITANT DISPERSERS
  1) Use
  2) Safety factors
  3) Care

h. CHEMICAL SPRAYS
  1) Types
  2) Dispensers
  3) Use
  4) Safety factors
  5) Care

i. GAS MASK
  1) TYPE
    a)
    b)
  2) USE
    a)
    b)
    c)
  3) CARE
    a)
    b)
    c)

j. TACTICAL EMPLOYMENT IN GENERAL
  1)
  2) Consideration of target nature
    a)
    b)
    c)

       d)
       e)
   3)
   4)
k. TACTICAL DEPLOYMENT
   1) PERSONNEL
      Sample situations:
l. FIRST AID
   1)
   2)
      a) EYES
         1.1)
         1.2)
      b) SKIN
         1.1)
         1.2)
      c) CLOTHING
         1.1)
      d) NOSE AND CHEST
         1.1)
         1.2)
m. DECONTAMINATION
   1)
   2)
   3)
   4)
   5)
n. REVIEW

TEAR GAS AND CHEMICAL SPRAY
CHEMICAL AGENT

I. TACTICAL APPLICATION (FIELD), FIELD DEMON-
STRATION, PRACTICAL APPLICATION (SAFETY
STRESSED)

    1. TEAR GAS DISPENSERS

        a. Grenades

        b. Projectiles and cartridges

        c. Irritant dispensers

        d. Chemical sprays

        e. Gas gun

        f. Grenade launchers

    2. USE OF PROTECTIVE MASK

        a.

        b.

        c.

    3. DECONTAMINATION

        a.

        b.

        c.

        d.

            1)

            2)

    4. TACTICAL DEPLOYMENT–SIMULATION
EXERCISE

        a.

        b.

        c.

            1)

            2)

            3)

    5. FINAL EXAMINATION–SIMULATION EXERCISE

    6. CRITIQUE OF SIMULATED EXERCISE

    7. TEAR GAS EXPOSURE

        a.

        b.

        c.

TRAINING BULLETIN # 116

SUBJECT: EVIDENCE
Compelling Nontestimonial Evidence by
Court Order.

SOURCE: (1) F.B.I., *Law Enforcement Bulletin,* Feb. 1971
        (2) *Miranda v. Arizona* (1966)
        (3) *Holt v. United States* (1910)
        (4) *Breithaupt v. Abram* (1957)
        (5) *Schmerber v. California* (1966)
        (6) *United States v. Wade* (1967)
        (7) *Gilbert v. California* (1967)
        (8) *People v. Arguello* (Calif. 1967)
        (9) *Graves v. Beto* (1969)
    (10) *United States v. Rudy* (1970)
    (11) *United States v. Doe* (1968)
    (12) *United States v. Vignera* (1969)
    (13) *United States v. Izzy* (1970)
    (14) F.B.I., *Law Enforcement Bulletin,* Apr. 1970
    (15) *United States v. Hammond* (1969)
    (16) *Doss v. United States* (1970)
    (17) *People v. Strauss* (N.Y. 1940)
    (18) Application of *Mackell* (N.Y. 1969)
    (19) *Williams v. United States* (1969)
    (20) *Orito v. United States* (1970)
    (21) *United States v. Scarpellino* (1969)
    (22) *United States v. Pahrms* (1970)
    (23) *Higgins v. Wainright* (1970)
    (24) *U.S. ex rel. O'Halloran v. Rundle* (1967)
    (25) *Davis v. Mississippi* (1969)
    (26) Johnson, Mr. Wilbur, San Mateo Co. D.D.A.
    (27) D.C.P.D., *Training Bulletin #88*, 3-5-70

PURPOSE: ROLL CALL TRAINING

AUTHOR: SUPERVISING CAPTAIN
DAVID A. HANSEN
3-3-71 STEEN #23

EVIDENCE—Compelling Nontestimonial Evidence by Court Order.

Introduction

A person under arrest may not be *forced to* undergo an unreasonable search and seizure, nor to confess to his own guilt, nor to speak or act without counsel in those circumstances in which he is entitled to counsel. Evidence obtained as a direct result of a violation of his Fourth, Fifth, and Sixth Amendment protections and guarantees is not admissible in court. (1) (2) *

Testimonial evidence may not be compelled. Nontestimonial evidence may be compelled, subject to guidelines here discussed.

Persons under arrest and, sometimes, those not under arrest can be forced to give evidence against themselves. The force is provided by the court.

A person under lawful arrest has no Constitutional right to refuse to provide nontestimonial evidence. He has no right to warnings such as the Miranda admonition, and in nontestimonial evidence matters, the right to counsel applies *only* to lineup cases. (6) (7) (27)

Departmental Policy

IN EVERY INSTANCE, WHETHER OR NOT REQUIRED BY LAW OR BY COURT DECISION, IT IS THE POLICY OF THE DALY CITY POLICE DEPARTMENT TO ADMONISH THE PERSON WHO REFUSES THE REQUEST OR COMMAND TO PERFORM OR SUBMIT (vis-a-vis NONTESTIMONIAL EVIDENCE) : THE REFUSAL CAN, AND PROBABLY WILL, BE USED AGAINST HIM IN COURT.

We should seek prosecutive counsel (advice of the D.A.) in any event; but, the import of this information is to stress that the suspect has no Constitutional right not to give nontestimonial evidence. (1)

---

*Citations on Cover Leaf

Nontestimonial Evidence

Some examples of nontestimonial evidence are listed here. They are examples and are not all-inclusive. An Officer in doubt about anything which he feels may constitute nontestimonial evidence should seek counsel.

1. Fingerprints and palmprints to compare with latents. (24)
2. Blood samples to be analyzed for alcoholic content. (4) (5) (8)
3. Hair samples for comparison with scene recovered hairs.
4. Photographs for identification.
5. Suspect's shoe to compare with prints found at the scene.
6. Donning of clothing or disguise of suspect for fit. (3) (6) (7) (15) (16)
7. Dried mud from suspect's shoe for scene sample comparison.
8. Dust from clothing for comparison to blown safe insulation.
9. Eyewitness identification by lineup. (6) (7) (15) (16)
10. Handwriting or handprinted samples (exemplars). (7) (10) (11) (12) (13) (14)

Obtaining Nontestimonial Evidence from the Suspect

1. We can ask the suspect to cooperate.
2. We can command the suspect to cooperate. (1)
3. We can use police muscle, in limited cases. (1)
4. We can use ruse or strategem, i.e. "tie this knot on this package for me." (1) (8)

Sometimes, however, these methods will not work or are not advisable. To muscle someone into a lineup would show the witnesses who the suspect really is. Forced handwriting will not produce the true script. (1) (8)

When these methods do not work or are not advisable, we can obtain and use the force of the court order to acquire the necessary and desired nontestimonial evidence. A court order, for example, can include an order to undergo a haircut and shave. (8) (17) (18) (19) (20) (21) (22) (23)

In some cases the court order can be made to apply to someone not yet under arrest. (25)

The Court Order

We can get a court order in much the same way as we obtain a search warrant. The order is executed and returned in the same fashion as is a search warrant.

In San Mateo County, we approach the situation with somewhat more circumspection than was required by the State of Colorado. We need *circumstances somewhat less than* those establishing *probable cause,* but more than a "shotgun, generalized approach. (26)

Contents of the order should include the following: (25)

1. Name and description of the suspect.
2. Names of the officers making the affidavit asking for issuance of the order.
3. The criminal offense with which we are concerned.
4. A mandate to the officer to detain the suspect only long enough to make the tests and comparisons.
5. The name and signature of the judge issuing the order.

Legal Protection of Suspect's Rights

Suspect, through his attorney, has the right to make a motion to suppress illegally or improperly obtained evidence.

TRAINING BULLETIN # 118

SUBJECT: WEAPONS INSPECTION AT ROLL CALL

SOURCE: S.O.P. (New)
(Illustrated on VTR Reel #3, 315-368)

PURPOSE: INSTRUCTIONAL GUIDE FOR
ROLL CALL SUPERVISORS

AUTHOR: TRAINING DIVISION
STEEN #23 3-17-71

Background

With the introduction of the S.O.P. weapons inspection was standardized and all personnel were instructed in this one procedure. There were only two (2) commands of execution, consisting of two (2) words each: *Inspection Arms,* and *Return Arms.*

In order to further simplify learned procedures in the handling of weapons, the new issue of the S.O.P. modified the weapons inspection drill in one point only to make it the same as the drill taught in range training. The weapon is unloaded, held, and reloaded in the same manner.

Frequent inspection and observation of the procedure will insure a uniform, reflexive, standardized, single response by all men to the commands of execution.

Observing a rule of leadership—The Troops Should Be Informed—the supervisor can inform his men that an inspection of weapons will be conducted. This information is provided formally or informally in several ways: "Today we are going to inspect weapons"; "Fall in on one line for inspection"; etc.

The supervisor can instruct on the correct procedure by outlining and spelling it out by the numbers, or by eliciting the thinking of the men, questioning individuals on the consecutive steps of the procedure, and then doing it. (VTR Film #3, 315-368 illustrates the procedure.)

Inspection Arms

On the command, "Inspection," the man unsnaps his holster and grasps his revolver by the grip with the trigger finger alongside the frame and *not* on the trigger. On the command, "Arms," the man frees his weapon from the holster, keeps the barrel pointed forward (in the case of a left-handed individual, he now transfers the weapon to his right hand), unlatches the cylinder latch with the thumb of his right hand while simultaneously opening the cylinder from the right side of the weapon, using the middle and ring fingers of his left hand, projects his middle and ring fingers through the frame and allowing the weapon to rest on the back of these fingers and the palm of the left hand. The man now releases his grip on the butt of the gun, ejects the bullets from the cylinder by depressing the ejector round with his left thumb while catching the ejected rounds in his cupped right hand, and visually verifies that the cylinder is empty, counting the number of rounds ejected (silently).

The man, standing at attention, now has his weapon supported on his left hand, his left elbow against his side, his left forearm at 45 degree angle across his chest, with his hand close below and on the nose/chin line. His right elbow is also against his side, his right forearm is extended forward horizontally, with his right hand cupping and displaying the ejected bullets for inspection.

If at any time the Officer should drop a bullet, he stops, recovers the dropped bullet, keeping the barrel always pointed to the front and avoiding the muzzle of any other weapon, and completes the inspection.

If the Supervisor should take an Officer's gun during the inspection, the Officer should drop his weapon hand to his side until the weapon is returned. When returned, the Officer recovers his weapon and assumes his prior position.

Return Arms

On the command, "Return," the man lowers his left hand and the gun, keeping the barrel pointed forward and downward, returns the bullets to the cylinder with his right hand, and, with the cylinder still open, regrips his gun by the butt with his right hand, drops his left hand to his side, and, with his right elbow into his side, extends his right forearm forward and downward at a 45 degree angle, with the trigger finger alongside the frame and *not* on the trigger. On the command, "Arms," the man maintains the position of his right hand and arm, reaches across with his left hand and closes the cylinder (in the case the man is left-handed, he now returns his weapon to his left hand, with the trigger finger alongside the frame), reholsters his weapon, resnaps his holster, and returns to a position of attention.

If at any time the Officer should drop a bullet, he stops, recovers the dropped bullet, and continues as before.

TRAINING BULLETIN # 101

SUBJECT: THE NOISY NEIGHBORHOOD PARTY
Commentary on Handling

SOURCE: *Law and Order,* June 1970, p. 33.
FOLLEY, Prof. V.L., Div. of Police and Public Admin.
Harrisburg, (Pa.) Area Community College.
Rewrite by STEEN #23, DCPD.

PURPOSE: ROLL CALL TRAINING

AUTHOR: TRAINING DIVISION
STEEN #23 7-13-70

The Problem

The noisy neighborhood party is a frequent complaint and Police response is within the realm of Police Authority and Responsibility. Citizens have a "right" to peace and quiet, and excessive noise of a disturbing character is considered a misdemeanor under municipal codes and the State law. (See Sections 19-4 C.C.D.C. and 415 P.C.)

However, the responding Officer must realize that this type of complaint is not a "cut-and-dry" problem. An arrest is not necessarily warranted, and, in fact, should be avoided. Diplomacy, sometimes called "Common Sense," and voluntary compliance should be the "order of the day." Frequently this complaint may reflect a deeper problem; a neighborhood "feud" may exist and the Police are called in to effect a reprisal. Such situations stress the need for diplomacy. The Police must avoid participation in a "feud." Diplomacy, understanding, and impartiality are guiding factors, and Police "action" is a last resort.

Assuming that the complaint is legitimate and pertinent information has been obtained by the Station Officer when he first received the telephoned complaint, this information should then be communicated to the Investigating Officer. Frequently the complainant will wish to remain annonymous, and common sense indicates that there is no reason to identify the complainant to the person hosting the party and thereby add more fuel to the neighborhood fire.

Having ascertained for himself that the party is indeed sufficiently loud that it could disturb neighbors, and having taken into account the time of day and any other special circumstances that may exist, the Investigating Officer, in a polite manner, should approach the party and attempt to engage the host in a quiet person-to-person conversation. He will explain the problem and request that the noise be toned down. The Officer, for example, may say, "I would appreciate it very much if you would do something about the excessive noise. Have a good time, but keep it reasonably quiet."

Usually this approach and request will be sufficient. If not, the Officer can explain that there is applicable law, and that action can be taken. Normally, however, the "authority-of-law" approach should be avoided, as voluntary compliance is the best solution.

TRAINING BULLETIN NO. 103

SUBJECT: THE 26" POLICE BATON, Instruction and Training Guide.*

SOURCE: S.O.P. 37.50, Supplemental Materials;
JORDAN, OFFICER R., #28, DCPD,
Physical Training Instructor;
Incidental Readings, Police and Military

PURPOSE: IN SERVICE INSTRUCTION & TRAINING GUIDE.

AUTHOR: TRAINING DIVISION
STEEN #23 7-1-70

I.   Introduction and Nomenclature
     A. Nomenclature and Definition of Terms
     B. Strengths and Weaknesses of the 26" Baton
     C. Uniforms and Uniform Use.
        1. Baton Holder
        2. Grommet
        3. Gloves
     D. Carry of the Baton

II. Striking Points
     A. Multiple Points, limited for reasons of:
        1. Danger
        2. Simplicity of Instruction and Use
        3. "Image" or Unfavorable Publicity
     B. Striking Points
        0. Head—not to be used
        1. Vagus Nerve
        2. Collar Bone
        3. Elbow and Wrist
        4. Colar Plexus
        5. Lower or Floating Rib
        6. Groin
        7. Knee
        8. Shin

---

*Employment of DCPD VTR Training Film is suggested.

III. Basic Stances
    A. Non-Combative Stances:
        1. Attention
        2. At Ease or Rest
            a. Without the Baton
            b. With Baton, a Ready Position
            c. Port Arms
    B. Combative Stances:
        1. On Guard
            a. Stance, Balance, Feet
            b. Position of Stick and Grip
        2. Thrust and Recovery
        3. Horse Stance

IV. Strokes and Combination of Strokes
    A. Concept of Stroke and Recovery
    B. Strokes:
        1. Thrust, Tip or Forward Thrust
        2. Vertical Butt Stroke
        3. Horizontal Stroke
            a. Avoid the overhead or baseball stroke
        4. Horizontal Butt Stroke
        5. Rear Thurst, Butt or Back Thrust
        6. Side Thrust, Employed from the Horse Stance

V. Guards
    A. Guards:
        1. Groin Block, Lower Butt Stroke
        2. Overhead
        3. Side, Right and Left
        4. Lower

VI. Parry

VII. Moving the Opponent

VIII. Movement and Utilization

IX. Comealongs
    A. Limited to 2 Comealongs applicable to the control situation

B. Comealongs:
   1. Chest-Collarbone Pressure Hold or Restraint
   2. Throat Pressure/Choke Hold or Restraint

X.   Defensive Butt Thrust from the Belt Carry

TRAINING BULLETIN #125

SUBJECT: DRUGS, DRUG ABUSE, EFFECTS, AND FIRST
         AID

SOURCE: THE AMERICAN NATIONAL RED CROSS,
        Drugs and their abuse.

PURPOSE: ROLL CALL TRAINING

AUTHOR: TRAINING DIVISION
        OFF. STEEN #23
        5-27-71

I. INTRODUCTION

A. Introduction

In response to the need for remedial advice concerning drug problems, the National Academy of Sciences-National Academy of Engineering, National Research Council, Division of Medical Sciences, Committee on Problems of Drug Dependence was requested by the American National Red Cross to define the information that should be given to the public as part of first aid education.

This material has been prepared to provide students of Red Cross First Aid courses and interested individuals with basic information about drugs and their effects, accepted medical uses when applicable, problems of overdose and abuse, and first aid.

—This same information can be used by the informed, trained, and professional Officer as the basis of valid performance in his duties, both in the stress-emergency life-saving function and in the nonstress informed-speaker representative of his Department. (23) —

B. Definitions

    1. DRUG. A substance that affects the function of the body or the mind when taken into the body or applied to its surface. Some drugs are readily available and are sold over-the-counter as home remedies. Most, however, are subject to some control or regulation for the protection of health. These latter are available only on a pre-

scription and are to be used only by his direction. Such use is accepted medical practice.

2. DRUG MISUSE. The use of drugs (a) for purposes or conditions for which they are unsuited or (b) for appropriate purposes but in improper dosage.

3. DRUG ABUSE. The excessive or persistent use of a drug without regard to accepted medical practice.

4. DRUG DEPENDENCE. The condition that results from drug abuse. It is described as the interaction between the drug and the body that involves an effect on the central nervous system. It is characterized by a behavioral response that always includes a compulsive desire to continue taking the drug, either to experience its effects or, sometimes, to avoid the discomfort of its absence. Dependence always involves psychic craving (psychic dependence) and, in some instances, physical, organic disturbance (physical dependence).

C. Identification of Drug Abuse

Almost any drug can be misused or abused; some drugs are commonly abused, constituting personal and public health problems, with social, economic, and legal implications.

In drug abuse emergencies, it is important that the signs and symptoms be identified. The type and amount of substance and the time it was taken should be determined, if possible.

It is sometimes difficult to distinguish between types of drugs taken by merely observing symptoms. This difficulty is increased when drugs are used in combination. The necessary clues to identification are provided by such apparatus as spoons, paper packs, eyedroppers, hypodermic needles, vials, or collapsible tubes. The presence of gelatin capsules, or pills, or of other drug containers and of needle marks or "tracks" on the body is also significant.

Information on the types of drugs taken, plus information on age, body size, and general condition and behavior, are needed by the drug abuse center or attending physician.

D. Classifications of Drugs

Drugs that are abused can be classified in many ways. The following listing is arranged for convenience, without regard to importance severity, or prevalence of abuse. Also, some of the groups overlap in one or more effect.

1. ALCOHOL (alcoholic beverages) ;
2. CANNABIS (marihuana and synthetics) ;
3. DEPRESSANTS (sedatives-hypnotics) ;
4. HALLUCINOGENS (natural and synthetic) ;
5. INHALANTS
6. NARCOTICS
7. STIMULANTS
8. TRANQUILIZERS

II. THE DRUGS

A. ALCOHOL

In this context, the term/classification *alcohol* refers to alcoholic beverages, the effects of which are related to their alcoholic content and to the level of alcohol in the blood resulting from their use. Alcoholic beverage is legal and widely accepted socially in the United States and many other countries. In spite of acceptance, prolonged abuse and consumption of large amounts of alcohol may cause great social and economic detriment, as well as physical damage, to the individual. Even a moderate amount of alcohol in combination with a barbiturate or a minor tranquilizer may be hazardous.

1. Effects

Alcohol is a depressant, affecting first the higher reasoning areas of the brain perhaps with a feeling of relaxation or, in the company of others, with a sense of exhilaration and conviviality due to the release of inhibitions. Later, motor activity, motor skills, and coordination are disrupted, and with deepening intoxication other bodily processes are disturbed. Superficial blood vessels are dilated, causing a feeling of warmth even though the actual effect is an increased loss of body heat. Respiration decreases; consciousness wanes; coma (prolonged unconsciousness) and death may result.

2. Abuse

The drinker uses alcohol, among other reasons, as a psychological crutch. Thus, he may develop a psychic, and later a physical, dependence similar to that produced by the barbiturates.

There is a well-defined abstinence syndrome closely related to that described for the barbiturates. Delirium Tremens (DTs) is a major symptom complex of alcohol withdrawal.

The odor of alcohol on a person's breath is not necessarily an indication of intoxication. In addition to noting information on incoordination, disturbance of speech, and altered respiration, other means are commonly used to determine if the level of alcohol in the body equals that of legally defined intoxication. The drinker is often unaware of detriment to his normal skills and should be restrained from activity requiring such skills, particularly driving.

3. First Aid

Alcohol intoxication is treated similarly whether it is due to an acute overdose or to prolonged abuse. If the person is sleeping quietly, his face is pink, his breathing normal, and his pulse regular, no immediate first aid is necessary.

If he shows such signs of shock as cold and clammy skin, rapid thready pulse, and abnormal breathing, or if he does not respond at all, obtain medical aid immediately. Maintain an open airway, give artificial respiration if indicated, and maintain body heat. If he is unconscious, place him in the coma position so that secretions may drool from the mouth. This position will usually allow for good respiration.

The *Coma Position.* Lying on one side, level, lower side of face resting on bicep area of the lower arm and the forearm-wrist-hand area of the upper arm. The upper half of the body tends to face downward. The airway should be cleared and open.

The intoxicated person may be violent and obstreperous and will need handling to prevent him from harming himself and others.

The alcoholic should be encouraged to seek help from Alcoholics Anonymous or from a drug abuse treatment center.

B. CANNABIS (Marihuana and THC)

Cannabis sativa is an herbaceous annual plant that grows wild in temperate climates in many parts of the world. The various forms of the drug are frequently referred to as cannabis, although the official definition states that "cannabis is the flowering or fruiting tops of the cannabis plant from which the resin has not been extracted." Marijuana usually consists of crushed cannabis leaves and flowers and often twigs. It varies greatly in the content of active material. Hashish is a preparation of cannabis resin, which is squeezed or scraped from the plant top and is generally five or more times as potent as marihuana. Marihuana is smoked; hashish may be smoked but it is also commonly made into a confection or beverage.

—THC (Tetra-hydro-cannabinol) is the laboratory used synthetic which is frequently made radioactive for medical research into the effects of marihuana, its flow, absorption, concentration, and retention in the human system. (23) —

1. Effects

The use of cannabis in medical practice is not presently recognized (-Exception is noted for European medical research particularly with THC as noted above. (23)

The effects here to be described are those experienced in abuse. These effects are dose-related: that is, the effects are dependent upon the content of active material —tetrahydrocannabinols in particular. The impression that marihuana is a harmless drug has been fostered by the low content of active material in American samples; however, use of the more potent hashish is increasing.

The immediate physical effects of smoking one or more marihuana cigarettes include:

Throat irritation;

Increased heart rate;

Reddening of the eyes;

Occasional dizziness, incoordination, or sleepiness;

and Increased appetite.

The psychological effects vary from individual to individual and with the amount of the drug taken. Among the effects described by users are feelings of exhilaration, hilarity, and conviviality. There is a distortion of time and space perception, and there may be disturbance of psychomotor activity, which would impair driving and other skills.

2. Abuse (Red Cross does not include this paragraph, so denominated, but does note the first paragraph, below.)

In some individuals and with excessive use of the drug, a psychotoxic reaction, resembling a bad trip on LSD, may occur. Many persons try marihuana once or twice and then abandon it; some use it intermittently, usually in the company of others; and many others use the drug continually. Marihuana can produce psychic dependence, but there is no evidence of physical dependence, and no withdrawal symptoms follow discontinuance.

—It must be noted here however, that reliable European and U.S. research by doctors and psychologists reports that heavy and particularly long term users do suffer change which is recognizable to them and observers. Such changes include those noted for alcohol: limits on the higher reasoning areas, disinterest in self, loss of ambition, etc. The noted changes last significantly longer than the alcoholic hangover.— (23)

3. First Aid

There is no need for emergency treatment unless a psychotoxic reaction develops, and then the approach is the same as that for a bad LSD Trip.

—The heavy, long-term, or frequent user should also be urged to consult with a drug abuse center as would be the case of an alcoholic.— (23)

C. Depressants (sedatives-hypnotics)

Depressants (downers) are drugs that act upon the nervous system, promoting relaxation and sleep. Chief among these drugs are the barbiturates, the more important of which are:

Phenobarbital (goofballs) ;
Pentobarbital (yellow jackets) ;
Amobarbital (blue devils) ; and,
Secobarbital (red devils) .

Closely related are the nonbarbiturate sedatives, some of which are:

Glutethimide (Doriden®) ;
Chloral hydrate (knockout drops) ; and,
Paraldehyde.

1. Effects

The usual therapeutic dose of barbiturates does not relieve pain but has a calming, relaxing effect, which promotes sleep.

Reactions include:

Relief of anxiety and excitement;
Tendency to reduce mental and physical activity;
and, Slight decrease in breathing.

Barbiturates are used to reduce the frequency of convulsions in epileptics, and one in particular—Pentothal®—is given intravenously as a preoperative sedative. An overdose of barbiturates produces unconsciousness, deepening to a coma, from which the victim cannot be roused. Barbiturates are frequently involved in accidental or intentional suicide.

Some accidental poisonings occur when a person becomes confused as a dose of barbiturates starts to take effect and he inadvertantly takes a second dose. Another cause of accidental poisoning is the mutual enhancement of effect that takes place when a barbiturate is taken in conjunction with alcohol. This combination can be lethal, even in small amounts.

2. Abuse

Barbiturates are commonly abused in two ways: (1) the barbiturate is taken in increasing amounts by persons who have developed tolerance to the drug, and thus larger and larger doses are required if the desired effects are to be felt; (2) for a thrill, it is injected as an alternate to other drugs that are being abused, particularly amphetamines.

Barbiturates can produce both psychic and physical dependence.

Abrupt discontinuance of barbiturate administration to the dependent person causes the following characteristic withdrawal symptoms:

Restlessness, insomnia, tremors;

Muscular twitching;

Nausea and vomiting;

Convulsions; and,

Delusions and hallucinations.

The convulsions and the psychotic symptoms seldom occur at the same time: the convulsions are likely to occur on the second or third day of withdrawal; the delusions and hallucinations a little later. The other symptoms usually occur within 24 hours of withdrawal.

If the individual is not treated the symptoms last about a week.

Abrupt withdrawal of barbiturates is dangerous. Withdrawal should take place gradually and under medical supervision.

The dependent person should be persuaded to get help from a physician or drug abuse treatment center.

3. First Aid

Maintain an open airway and give artificial respiration if indicated.

Maintain body temperature.

Get the victim to a physician or hospital as soon as possible.

D. Hallucinogens

Hallucinogens are drugs that are capable of producing mood changes, which are frequently of a bizarre character; disturbances of sensation, thought, emotion, and self-awareness; alteration of time and space perception; and both illusions and delusions.

The most important hallucinogen is LSD (lysergic acid diethylamide). Some of the others are:

Mescaline;
Psilocybin;
Morning glory seeds; and,
Synthetics.

1. Effects; 2. Abuse

Since none of these substances presently has accepted medical use, the effects described are those experienced in abuse.

Abuse of hallucinogens is of the spree type: the drug is taken intermittently, though perhaps as often as several times a week. Many persons develop a psychic drive for repetition of the experience, but physical dependence does not develop. The effects may often seem pleasurable and rewarding, but they may also be very unpleasant (a "bad trip"), even in the same individual.

LSD, for example, is likely to produce these physical effects:

Increased activity through its action on central nervous system;
Increased heart rate;
Increased blood pressure;
Increased body temperature;
Dilated (enlarged) pupils; and,
Flushed face.

The psychological effects of hallucinogens in general are highly variable and unpredictable. They include an emergence into consciousness of previously suppressed ideas, a strong emotional feeling, an impression of astonishingly lucid thought, a feeling of insight and creativity, and an intensification of sensory impressions.

Changes in sensation may also be involved (sounds are "seen," ordinary things appear beautiful, colors seem to be heard).

A feeling of cosmic oneness and profound religious awareness and a mood of joy and peace may also mark the use of hallucinogens.

In the "bad trip," or freakout, there is an intense experience of fear or nightmarish terror to the point of panic. Other undesirable effects are:

Complete loss of emotional control;
Paranoid delusions;
Hallucinations;
Profound depression; and,
Tension and anxiety.

Disordered social behavior may also occur. Because of the delusions and disordered sensations, the user may think he is immune from harm or perhaps able to fly and may suffer severe physical injury.

Flashbacks (sensory replay of a previous trip) are associated with the use of hallucinogenic drugs such as LSD and may occur months after the drug has been taken. They may be severe or simply a feeling of dizziness or a temporary blackout.

3. First Aid

The person on a trip, good or bad, needs careful attention, reassurance, and protection from bodily harm or the results of his antisocial behavior.

Talk him down from his disturbing experience in quiet and safe surroundings. Get the victim to a physician or a hospital as soon as possible. Preferably, two persons should accompany him.

E. INHALANTS

Occasional self-administration of volatile substances such as ether or chloroform, in order to experience intoxication, is a very old practice.

In recent years, inhalation of a wide variety of substances, a practice commonly referred to as glue-sniffing, has become widespread among young people in their early teens.

The substances inhaled include:

Fast-drying glue or cement (model airplane glue) ;
Many paints and lacquers and their thinners and removers;
Gasoline;
Kerosene;
Lighter and dry-cleaning fluids; and,
Nail polish and remover.

The usual methods of inhaling are to hold over the nose and mouth a cloth with some of the substance on it or to cover the head with a paper or plastic bag containing a quantity of the substance.

1. Effects

The effects resulting from use of inhalants are those experienced in abuse.

2. Abuse

Reactions are:

Initial excitment, resulting from release of inhibitions;
Irritation of the respiratory passages;
Unsteadiness; and,
Drunkenness with growing depression, which deepens even to unconsciousness.

A serious potential danger accompanies waning consciousness: failure to remove the bag from the inhaler's head may result in suffocation.

Some of the propellants in the aerosols that are inhaled are toxic to the heart and can cause death by alteration in the rhythm of the heartbeat. This situation requires prompt and intensive medical attention.

Persistent use of inhalants may cause some psychic dependence and may produce pathological changes in the liver and other organs.

3. First Aid

If a person is found with a bag or other apparatus over his head, remove it immediately.

If breathing stops, apply artificial respiration.

Obtain medical assistance immediately.

F. NARCOTICS

Narcotics refer in general to opium and specifically to:

Preparations of opium, such as paregoric;

Substances found in opium (morphine and codeine) ;

Substances derived from morphine (heroin, Dilaudid, etc.); and,

Synthetic (laboratory-made) substances that have morphine-like effects (meperidine or Demerol®; methadone or Dolophine®, etc.) .

"In late 1970, federal laws governing the control of narcotics appropriately excluded cocaine and marihuana from the narcotics classification. Cocaine is a stimulant that effects the central nervous system, and marihuana is a mood- and sense-altering substance."

1. Effects

The therapeutic dose of narcotics relieves pain and reaction to pain, calms anxiety, and promotes sleep. Common reactions to morphine, heroin, and other morphine-like agents include:

Reduction of awareness of pain;

Quieting of tension and anxiety;

Decrease in activity;

Promotion of sleep;

Decrease in breathing and pulse rate; and,

Reduction of hunger and thirst.

Some unpleasant reactions to narcotics include sweating, dizziness, nausea, vomiting, and constipation.

An overdose of narcotics results in the following conditions:

Lethargy and increasing reduction in activity and awareness;

Sleep deepening to coma;

Increasing depression of breathing to the point of respiratory failure;

Profuse sweating;

Fall in temperature;

Muscle relaxation; and,

Pinpoint pupils (except with meperidine).

2. Abuse

The continued administration of a narcotic produces both psychic and physical dependence. Discontinuing the drug causes the appearance within six to twenty-four hours of the characteristic, recognizable withdrawal symptoms, including:

Nervousness, restlessness, anxiety;

Tears and a runny nose;

Sweating, hot and cold flashes, gooseflesh;

Yawning;

Muscular aches and pains in legs, back, and abdomen;

Nausea, vomiting, diarrhea (uncontrollable and continuous);

Loss of appetite, loss of weight;

Dilated (enlarged) pupils;

Increased breathing, blood pressure, and body temperature; and

Intense craving for the drug (for a fix).

If withdrawal symptoms are in evidence, they may be promptly relieved by a dose of the same drug or of another drug in the same group.

There is little the lay person can do for the individual in withdrawal except to reassure him and to persuade him to go to a drug treatment center or a physician.

Other problems associated with the use/abuse of narcotics are infection, resulting from the use of unsterile needles; the possibility of developing hepatitis; and malnutrition and dental caries from neglect of dietary and hygienic practices.

3. First Aid

Arouse the victim, if possible, by lightly slapping him with a cold, wet towel and try to get him on his feet.

Maintain an open airway and apply artificial respiration if indicated.

Maintain body temperature.

Avoid rough treatment of the victim.

Reassure the victim and seek medical assistance as soon as possible.

G. STIMULANTS

Stimulants (uppers) and used to increase mental activity and to offset drowsiness and fatigue. The most commonly abused stimulants are:

Amphetamine: Benzedrine (bennies, pep pills) ;

Dextroamphetamine: Dexedrine (dexies) ;

Methamphetamine: Methedrine (meth, speed, crystal) ; and,

Methylphenidate: Ritalin.

All of these drugs act similarly and are described here as exemplified by amphetamine.

Caffeine and cocaine are included among the stimulants. Caffeine, a constituent of coffee, tea, and other beverages, may produce a very mild psychic dependence, but it does not cause personal or social damage. Cocaine, used medically as a local anesthetic, is a powerful central nervous system stimulant.

1. Effects

In therapeutic doses, amphetamine produces the following effects:

Alertness;
Wakefulness;

Relief from fatigue; and

A feeling of well-being.

Mental and physical performance may increase to some extent. Amphetamine reduces hunger and has been widely used for this purpose, although the effect is not well sustained, and the feelings of alertness and wakefulness wear off. Amphetamine increases blood pressure, breathing, and general bodily activity. Tolerance to the effects of amphetamine can develop to a high degree, which results in a demand for larger doses.

An overdose of amphetamine may produce toxic effects when taken orally, but these effects are more common when amphetamine is taken intravenously.

Use of amphetamine as an antiobesity agent (diet pill) has limited value, and there is little recognized medical need for this drug, although it is occasionally used in treating narcolepsy (uncontrollable desire for sleep) and hyperkinetic (overactive) states.

2. Abuse

Amphetamine abuse can produce strong psychic dependence and a pronounced degree of tolerance but not physical dependence. Prolonged administration of oral doses for diet or fatigue control, because of the accompanying sense of well-being, frequently leads to abuse as the doses are increased in an effort to maintain an effect. This abuse produces a psychic dependence on the drug, but withdrawal should be possible without serious incident.

In recent years, a form of amphetamine abuse involving repeated intravenous injection of the drug (usually Methedrine or Dexedrine) has developed. Called a speed run, it is accompanied by considerable risk to the individual and the people around him. The pattern of abuse begins with several days of repeated injections, which increase in size and frequency. The daily total sometimes reaches more than one hundred times the initial dose. Initially, the user may feel energetic, talkative, enthusiastic, happy, and confident. He does not sleep and usually eats little or nothing. After a few days, unpleasant symptoms appear and increase as the dose increases. These symptoms include:

> Confusion;
> Disorganization;
> Compulsive repetition of small, meaningless acts;
> Irritability;
> Suspiciousness;
> Fear;
> Hallucinations and delusions, which may become paranoid; and,
> Aggressive and antisocial behavior, which may endanger others.

The run, which usually lasts less than a week, is abruptly terminated. The abuser is left exhausted. He sleeps—sometimes for several days—and on awakening, he is emotionally depressed, lethargic, and extremely hungry. Shortly, another run is begun and the cycle is repeated. There is little that can be done for the victim except to protect him against injury and to seek psychiatric help for the delusions and hallucinations.

Abuse of cocaine may take a form similar to the speed run, with rapid repeated intravenous injections followed by psychotoxic symptoms similar to those characteristic of amphetamine, particularly delusions of a paranoid nature. Another cocaine abuse practice is the taking of the drug alternately or concurrently with heroin. In this combination, cocaine provides the up and heroin the down.

Cocaine abuse results in strong psychic dependence but not physical dependence.

3. First Aid

Protect the victim against injury.

Maintain an open airway and administer artificial respiration if indicated.

Maintain body temperature.

Obtain psychiatric help for the victim's delusions and hallucinations.

H. TRANQUILIZERS

Agents in this category are commonly referred to as *major* and *minor* tranquilizers.

Major tranquilizers include phenothiazines (chlorpromazine, for example), and reserpine. They are used in treating mental disease to calm psychotic patients. They have not produced dependence, but overdosage of these drugs produce a deepening state of unconsciousness, a fall in body temperature and blood pressure, and eventual respiratory failure. The effects produced by an overdose are prolonged, and the victim must be watched carefully as long as severe central nervous system depression continues.

Minor tranquilizers are used to calm anxiety and other feelings of stress and excitement without producing sleep. At high dose levels their effects are virtually indistinguishable from the effects of sedative-hypnotics. Common examples of minor tranquilizers are:

Meprobamate (Miltown, Equanil);
Chlordiazepoxide (Librium);
Ethchlorvynol; (Placidyl); and,
Diazepam (Valium).

Some tranquilizers are used in treating chronic alcoholism, but in effect this practice represents substitution of one depressant drug for another. These drugs are useful in treating acute alcohol withdrawal.

Prolonged administration of a minor tranquilizer, with a tendency to increase the dose, may result in psychic and physical dependency. The characteristics of dependence on minor tranquilizers and the related withdrawal symptoms are similar to those of barbiturates.

3. First Aid

Arouse the victim, if possible, by lightly slapping him with a cold, wet towel and try to get him on his feet.

Maintain an open airway; artificially respirate indicated.

Maintain body temperature.

Get victim to physician, hospital, or drug abuse center as soon as possible.

TRAINING BULLETIN #126

SUBJECT: PROVIDING SERVICE WHILE ASKING THE CITIZEN TO WAIT.

SOURCE: STAFF BUREAU

PURPOSE: TRAINING, COMMUNICATIONS PERSONNEL

AUTHOR: TRAINING DIVISION
STEEN #23 7-8-71

Introduction:

Service is the name of the game. We are a service organization. When a citizen comes to us in person or by using his phone, he has a problem and has turned to us to provide the answer. Whatever we do at every step of the problem solving process is the service we provide, the reason for our agency existence.

How can service be given when the "hold" button is used on the phone? How can service be given when a person is told to sit down and wait, "An Officer will be in."? How can service be provided when a call is "stacked"?

The Phone "Hold" Trauma

You've had the experience. Evaluate this experience of yours with that you're now transfering to the person on the other end of your phone line. How long would you "hold," particularly when what you have to do is urgent?

You don't enjoy the experience of trying to call a Police agency, for information that an Officer is requesting, to be greeted: "XX Police Department. Please Hold." This is pure frustration. This is also pure frustration for the citizen calling Daly City Police.

Phones should be answered immediately, at least by the second ring. Contact between the caller and this Department is established.

An initial understanding of the actual emergency nature of the call should be obtained. If the call is of a nonemergency nature, then an initial explanation for placing the call on "hold" should be given. The simplest explanation of two or three words that an emergency is in progress, or that you must place the call on "hold" will suffice. If the caller can understand your problem he will wait with patient understanding; if the caller can't understand why he is being deferred, he will wait with irritation if not anger.

IN EVERY CASE, GET BACK TO THE CALLER. MAINTAIN COMMUNICATION AND UNDERSTANDING. THIS IS PROVIDING SERVICE.

The Sit-Down and Wait

Frequently the person seeking a solution for his problems will take the extra effort to come in person to the Police Department for help. When investigation is indicated, the most appropriate person to conduct the investigation is the person's own personal Officer. This Officer is the District Officer, the Officer who has daily contact with this person's problems, the particular area involved. This is the information, which, if given to the person at the Complaint Desk, will create an understanding and a wait with patience. DON'T STOP.

Go Further! Provide the District Officer's name. Give an approximate time of arrival.

While waiting, this person will see a number and variety of Police personnel passing by. If he knows, however, that he is waiting for a specific Officer JONES, he won't wonder if the Officer, the Sergeant, and Captain, or the Cadet is the one coming to help him, only to see him pass by, or wonder why this other Policeman isn't helping him.

DON'T STOP! If an emergency or other interruption causes a delay of the Officer's arrival at the Complaint Desk, explain this cause of delay. The patiently waiting victim will understand.

SERVICE AND CONTINUITY OF SERVICE IS PROVIDED.

The "Stacked" Call

It is not uncommon, during peak work periods, to have to "stack" a nonemergency call pending the availability of the district Officer. We know the reasons for assigning calls to the district Officer. We know which calls require priority assignment. Does the caller with his problem know the reasons? To him his problem is important; it's important enough to him that he bothered to call. The caller is entitled to service; he is entitled to know how long and why he is asked to wait for the availability of the district Officer. TELL HIM!!

The District Officer is the caller's personal Officer. The District Officer has daily contact and familiarity with the caller's area and its problems. The District Officer can give him the best and more personalized service than any other Officer. TELL HIM!! Give him a name; use his badge number. This information gives the caller that feling and realization that an identified specialist is going to arrive and solve his problems. DON'T STOP! Tell the caller when he can specifically expect to have personal contact with his Officer. Don't say: "In about 20 minutes."; spell out what time it will be in 20 minutes. DON'T STOP!

You know, from established procedure, that, if it is necessary to "stack" a call for an hour, you are to advise your watch commander. DON'T WAIT! If the time you have appointed is arriving and there is still no district Officer available, recontact your caller; preserve the contact originally made; make a decision as to what you are going to do; communicate this to the caller.

THUS IS SERVICE PROVIDED TO THE CITIZEN WHOM YOU HAVE ASKED TO WAIT.

TRAINING BULLETIN #127

SUBJECT: INSANITY, The Extra Male or Y Chromosome.

SOURCE: WEEKLY LAW DIGEST, Vol. 35 No. 7, 2-15-71
People v. Tanner, 13 CA3 596, Los Angeles, 217 PC.

PURPOSE: ROLL CALL TRAINING

AUTHOR: TRAINING DIVISION
STEEN #23 7-13-71

Introduction:

Considerable interest and speculation arose as a result of this case, involving 217PC, Assault With Intent to Commit Murder, when TANNER wanted to plead not guilty by reason of insanity, in that he possessed an "extra male or Y chromosome" which "tends to make such persons "exhibit certain aggressive behaviorial traits."

In this case the question was for Court determination because it arose on motion to change plea of guilty to a not guilty-insanity status.

Conclusion:

Appelate Court held in this case that Trial Court did not err in concluding that Defendant's voluminous evidence was not clear and convincing (as to this basis for finding criminal insanity).

TRAINING BULLETIN #128

SUBJECT: FELONY DRUNK DRIVING, Alcohol vs. NARCOTICS

A Substantial Legal Difference and Felony-Murder.

SOURCE: WEEKLY LAW DIGEST, Vol. 37 No. 7, 2-15-71

People v. Calzada, 13 CA3 603, Santa Barbara, 187PC.

PURPOSE: ROLL CALL TRAINING

AUTHOR: TRAINING DIVISION

STEEN #23 7-13-71

Introduction:

It is established under California law that if a death results from the commission of a felony a conviction of Felony-Murder can result also.

Under this law, the *Ireland* and *Wilson* cases were decided and held: the felony-murder rule does not apply where the underlying felony is a necessary ingredient of a homicide. However it does apply where the underlying felony is independent of the homicide.

Facts of This Case:

CALZADA, driving under the influence of narcotics, crossed the planted divider of a four-lane highway, crashed into an oncoming car, killed the driver. He was charged with 192(3) PC-Vehicular Manslaughter, 23105VC-Narcotic Drunk Driving, and 187/189PC-Second Degree Felony Murder.

23105VC—Narcotic Drunk Driving:

Addicted to, or driving under the influence of narcotic is felony.

23101VC—Alcoholic Drunk Driving and Injury:

Driving under the influence of alcohol, plus violation of the law, plus bodily injury to another is felony.

Conclusion:

The felony of 23105VC is complete when driving commences

on the highway and is independent of the homicide. Charge 187/189PC.

The felony of 23101VC, although not decided here, is not complete until injury to another occurs. If homicide results the felony is not independent of the homicide. No 187/189PC.

TRAINING BULLETIN #129

SUBJECT: VEHICULAR THEFT, THE PROBLEM AND AIDS TO SOLUTION OF

SOURCE: CHP TRAINING BULLETIN #1 (Rev. 6-1-71)

PURPOSE: ROLL CALL TRAINING

AUTHOR: TRAINING DIVISION, STEEN #23 7-14-71

The Vehicle Theft Problem:

Through March 1971, there were 10.8 million private motor vehicles registered with DMV: 8.9 million autos; 1.5 million trucks; and 0.4 million motorcycles.

During 1970 there were 137,660 reported vehicle thefts in California, 14,577 of which were motorcycles.

The recovery rate for all vehicles was about 84 percent. The recovery rate for motorcycles was only 35.9 percent, many of which were total losses, the recovery being only a transmission, a motor, or a frame.

Motorcycle theft and recovery problems are more severe due to the expected problems of easy theft and concealment. These problems are further intensified by lack of identification information on the part of Officers and inadequte registration procedures by DMV. The percentage of incorrectly registered motorcycles varies from 20 to 55 percent.

Aids To The Solution of The Problem—Tips to Identification of Theft:

1. The Unusual Driver—The Violator; The Reckless; The Over-Cautious.
2. The Over-Solicitous Volunteer—He answers questions before they are even asked.
3. The Ignition Key Without Teeth.
4. The Missing, Punched, and Battered Ignition Lock.
5. Can the Driver Stop and Start the Car? The Starter Motor Jumper.
6. The Ignition Key that Won't Unlock the Door.

7. Does the Driver's Identification Relate to the Vehicle Identification?
8. Does the License Identification Relate to the Vehicle?
9. Are the License Plates Secure and Unaltered?
10. Signs of Forced Entry.
11. Signs of VIN plate tampering.
12. Frequent Checks of Typical and Local Recovery Areas— Check Street and Off-Street Areas (carports, parking lots, and shopping centers.)
13. Close Inspection of Supposed Specially Constructed Vehicles—

Some "outlaw" motorcycle gangs specialize in "hot" machines. With motorcycle numbers, bear in mind: Good Numbers Look Good; Bad Numbers Look Bad. There is no valid reason for grind marks, chisel or punch marks, uneven or over-stamping, or fresh paint or chrome in number areas only.

14. Is the "Bill of Sale" Genuine?

YOUR EYES AND KNOWLEDGE COMBINED WITH COMMON SENSE ARE YOUR WEAPONS!! USE THEM! USE THEM FREQUENTLY!!

(CHP, NATB, and Local Law Enforcement have prepared a series of Vehicle Theft Training Bulletins on identification of motorcycles and automobiles. Future bulletins will cover trucks, tractors, trailers, and recreation vehicles.)

TRAINING BULLETIN #129A

SUBJECT: VEHICLE THEFT, MOTORCYCLES

SOURCE: CHP TRAINING BULLETIN # (Rev. 6-25-71)

PURPOSE: ROLL CALL TRAINING

AUTHOR: TRAINING DIVISION, STEEN #23 7-23-71

The Motorcycle Theft Problem:

Motorcycle theft and recovery problems are more severe than in automobile thefts and recoveries due to the ease of theft and transportation and concealment, and the confusion existing in registration procedures and requirements.

Overall vehicle recovery was about 84 percent in 1970. Motorcycle recovery, during the same time, was only 35.9 percent.

All Officers should carefully observe the driving habits of motorcycle riders and, whenever violations of the law are observed, appropriate enforcement action should be taken.

During the enforcement stop, a complete examination of the motorcycle, the driver's identification, and the registration documents should be made. If an alteration of frame or engine number is observed, the vehicle is to be impounded as an illegal vehicle under 10751 CVC and 537e PC. Written authorization is required from DMV for affixing other numbers or marks.

A list of applicable Vehicle Code sections pertaining to motorcycles is enumerated in Part I, below.

PART I

A. TRAFFIC LAWS HAVING APPLICATION TO MOTORCYCLES AND MOTOR-DRIVEN CYCLES

1. §400VC Motorcycle-Defined: Motor vehicle (other than tractor) ; seat or saddle for the rider; not more than 3 wheels on the ground (except for 4 wheels with functional side-car) ; weighing less than 1500 pounds.

2. §405VC Motor-Driven Cycle—Defined: Every motorcycle

(including motor scooter) producing less than 15 gross brake horsepower, and bicycle with motor attached.

3. §2420VC Motorcycle—Gross Brake Horsepower; Certified by manufacturer to CHP, or illegal for dealer to sell.

4. §2806VC Vehicle and Equipment Inspection: Any Police Officer, with reasonable cause to believe vehicle not equipped as required, or unsafe, may require stop, inspection, and appropriate test.

5. §4150.2VC Application for Motorcycle Registration: a) true full name and business or residence address of owners; county of residence; c) description, including make, model, bodytype, number of cylinders, motor and frame numbers (DMV to maintain cross-index; and, tracing of the motor number.

6. §4454VC Registration Card Kept With Vehicle: original or facsimile.

7. §4462VC Valid Registration Card, Present for Examination: Driver to present on demand of Peace Officer; display or present phony.

8. §4850VC Issuance of Plates: one plate issued for motorcycles.

9. §5019VC Special Plates, Motorcycles and Trailers: "Horseless Carriage," "Ham Radio" and "Press" special plates not for cycles.

10. §5200VC Display of Plates: Issued single plate attached to rear.

11. §9268VC Motorcycles—Original Registration: additional $1.00 fee.

12. §10751VC Altered I.D. Numbers: No person shall knowingly buy, receive, dispose of, sell, offer for sale, or have in his possession any vehicle or component thereof from which a manufacturer's serial or i.d. number, motor number. . . , or any identification mark or number placed thereon under assignment from DMV has been removed, defaced, covered, altered, or destroyed for the

purpose of concealing or misrepresenting the identity or gross weight of vehicle or component. When any such property comes into the custody of a peace officer, he shall hold it, subject to the order of the magistrate. . . . as provided in 1419PC.

12A §537ePC Purchase, Sale, Receipt, Disposal, Concealment, or Possession of Articles from which I.D. Removed: knowing of. . . .bicycle. . . .firearm. . . .or any mechanical or electrical device, appliance, contrivance, material, piece of apparatus or equipment. . . . misdemeanor.

13. §12509VC Instruction Permits: Alone, not during hours of darkness, not on freeways, no passengers except licensed instructor (11100VC) or Qualified Instructor (18252.2 Ed. Code) .

14. §12804(b)VC Class 4 Motorcycle Licenses: Or endorsement to Class 1, 2, or 3 License; However a valid class 1, 2, or 3 License, issued prior to 11-13-68, is valid for motorcycle until expiration.

15. §21960 Freeways: posted freeways can prohibit use by pedestrians, bicycles, or motor-driven cycles.

16. §22502VC Curb Parking: Motorcycles to have one wheel or fender touching the curb (righthand) ; no curb or barrier, then parallel right-hand parking.

17. §24004VC Unlawful operation after notice by Officer: If unsafe or not equipped, no operation, except to residence or business of owner or driver, or to a garage, until conforming.

18. §24005VC Sale, Transfer or Installation of Unlawful Equipment: Unlawful to sell, offer for sale, lease, install, or replace, for self or as or through agent or employee. . . .any kind of equipment not in conformity with code or regulations.

19. §24253VC Taillamps Which Remain Lighted: Motorcycles manufactured and first registered after 1-1-71 must have lights which operate without motor for at least one-fourth hour. (Taillamps)

20. §24406VC Multiple Beams: Driver must be able to select at will between high or low beams during darkness (automatic is ok) ;

21. §24408VC Beam Indicator: When multiple beams, indicator is a must; can't exceed 2cp; not to show to front or sides.

22. §24410VC Single Beams: applies to vehicles mfg'd. and sold prior to 9-19-40.

23. §24600VC Taillamps: one minimum, red, plainly visible 500 feet (1000 feet if manufactured after 1-1-69 and between 15" & 72" up.)

24. §24601VC License Plate Lamp: White, operated by taillamp switch, license to be clearly legible at 50 feet in darkness.

25. §24603VC Stoplamps: one minimum, red or amber, plainly visible and understandable from 300 feet day and night, actuated by the foot brake (and, manufactured after 1-1-69 between 15" & 72" up). Multiple brake lights, rear of seat if additional to regular stop lamp can be used as turn signals.

26. §25451VC Acetylene Lamps: motorcycles can use for headlamp.

27. §25650VC Headlamps, motorcycle: one minimum, two maximum, lighted during darkness.

28. §25651VC Headlamps, motor-driven cycles: single or multi-beam type.

29. §26311VC Service Brakes on All Wheels: a) Every motor vehicle shall be equipped with service brakes on all wheels, except: 5) motorcycle sidecar; 6) motorcycles manufactured prior to 1966 need only one wheel to be braked. (24603 defines service brake as foot brake.)

30. §26453VC Condition of Brakes: Good Condition & Good Working Order.

31. §26454VC Control and Stopping Requirements: Adequate to control the movement of the vehicle and to stop and

hold the vehicle on the grade where being operated, under any conditions to stop the vehicle within 25 feet at 20 mph.

32. §26701VC Safety Glazing Material for Windshields: a) all vehicles manufactured after 1-1-36 must use safety glazing wherever glazing is used; b) motorcycles manufactured after 1-1-69 not operated with windshield unless of safety glazing; c) no red or amber glazing.

32A §26703VC Replacement of Glazing Material: Must be with safety glazing.

33. §26705VC Motorcycle Windshields: If used, must have safety glazing.

34. §26709VC Mirrors: Motorcycles subject to registration in this State must have one mirror providing 200 feet rear view to driver.

35. §27000VC Horns or Warning Devices: When operated on highway, every motor vehicle equipped with horn in good working order, capable of emitting sound audible under normal conditions at 200 feet.

36. §27150VC Mufflers: Every motor vehicle subject to registration shall at all times be equipped with an adequate muffler in constant operation and properly maintained to prevent excessive or unusual noise; no exhaust system to be equipped with cutout, bypass, etc.

37. §27151VC Modification of Exhaust System: No modification permitted which will amplify, or increase, motor noise above original muffler, which, itself, must comply with requirements of code.

38. §27155VC Fuel Tank Caps: no operation or parking on highway unless closed or covered with noncombustible.

39. §27600VC Fenders and Mudguards: (Applies to vehicle with 3 or more wheels.)

40. §27800VC Passengers: Equipment and Usage: Motorcycle passenger must have a seat securely fastened to machine behind driver and provided with footrests, which must be used by the passenger, or be in a *passenger* sidecar.

41. §27801VC Handlebar & Seat Requirements: Driver in seat must be able to touch ground with feet when seated; handlebars not more than 15" above seat where driver seated and depressed with his weight.

42. §27802VC Safety Helmet Regulations (Effective 6 months after DMV adopts helmet regulations): Helmets not to be sold or offered for sale for motorcycle driver or passenger use unless of approved type.

B. ALL OTHER PROVISIONS OR LAW GENERALLY APPLICABLE TO MOTOR VEHICLES ARE APPLICABLE TO MOTORCYCLES IN ADDITION TO THE SPECIFIC SECTIONS ABOVE.

REGISTRATION AND LICENSING LAWS APPLY TO ALL MOTOR-DRIVEN CYCLES INCLUDING BICYCLES WITH A MOTOR ATTACHED AND ONE-FOURTH MIDGET TYPE VEHICLES.

PART II

A. ALTERED MANUFACTURERS' NUMBERS. Whenever any alteration is found on a motorcycle identification number or numbers, several steps may be taken to provide a solid foundation for proper recovery and/or prosecution.

1. Impound the motorcycle for the authorization that is most applicable at the time.

   a. 22651(c) or 22653VC—Stolen report on file

      (1) Recovery of stolen vehicle.
      (2) Prosecution for 10851VC—Stolen Vehicle;
          Prosecution for 487PC—Grand Theft, Auto;
          Prosecution for 496PC—Receiving/Concealing.

   b. Impound for Evidence

      (1) The authority or the right to seize and hold evidence is historically an incident of sovereignty. The State of California is limited by the provisions of the Constitution of the State of California, treaties of the U.S., and the Constitution of the U.S. The limita-

tions on seizure are generally stated in Article 1, Section 19 of the Calif. Constitution;

"The right of the people to be secure in their persons, houses, papers, and effects, against unreasonable seizures and searches, shall not be violated. . . ."

Therefore, the State has the right to seize evidence so that it may successfully prove violations of the law provided that the seizure is not unreasonable.

When any vehicle which exhibits removed/ altered numbers comes to the attention of an Officer, he shall assure himself that there is reasonable and probable cause to believe a violation of the law exists.

The Officer has the right to make a reasonable inspection of the vehicle and/or component parts in an attempt to identify said vehicle or components.

If the vehicle has been reported stolen, the vehicle is to be seized and stored as provided in the Vehicle Code. After the evidence has been preserved, i.e. tape lifts, photographs, recovery of latent prints, the vehicle is to be returned to the rightful owner.

Component parts of a vehicle which exhibit removed/altered numbers, likewise may be seized.

If a vehicle or component parts with removed/altered numbers are not seized, Officers should obtain all possible facts which would aid in obtaining a search warrant and the future seizure of the vehicle or parts in question.

If, following inspection, the vehicle or component part thereof cannot be identified as having been stolen, it may have to be returned to the person who was in possession of it at the time seizure was effected, providing he has legal right thereto. The possessor of property is the legal owner absent any superior legal claim to ownership and absent legal prohibition of ownership. The necessary steps that a possessor must follow to obtain i.d. numbers and affix them to the vehicle are outlined in the Code (10750VC) and 1419PC (per 10751VC).

Whether violation of 10751VC exists is determined by the facts available to the Officer making the inspection and a reasonable cause to believe a violation of the law exists.

Evidentiary information, to be used in court proceedings, for procuring a search warrant, and to establish reasonable cause, can be obtained by the techniques and use of a field kit specified in II, C, below.

(2) There are generally three types of property which may be seized:

    (a) Anything which may be reasonable used as evidence for providing the commission of a crime or tending to prove such;

    (b) Fruits of a crime;

    (c) Contraband.

B. OBTAINING EVIDENCE AND INFORMATION FOR FURTHER INVESTIGATION AND PROSECUTION.

Whenever there is uncertainty as to the motorcycle's legality and/or commission of a crime, certain steps should be taken to provide a basis for a successful prosecution should this be necessary at a later date.

1. Obtain full and accurate information on subject and vehicle at the time of inspection. Do not rely solely on the suspect's statements. Verify your information by i.d. in his possession.

2. Designate where the vehicle can be located at what time and date.

3. Obtain a "Lift" on *all* visible *identification numbers.*

4. DOCUMENT YOUR REASONABLE CAUSE TO STOP AND IDENTIFICATION. ISSUE THE CITATION. If

a moving violation, the driver is identified and the vehicle is identified by documents which must be valid and must be in his possession.

C. A SUGGESTED FIELD KIT FOR MAKING "LIFTS" AND GATHERING PHYSICAL EVIDENCE

1. A "Lift" is a simple operation for retaining a fingerprint-type record of number impressions.

   Items needed are:
   a. Cleaning solvent of a nonoil base type, such as lacquer thinner or acetone (fingernail polish remover) ;
   b. Clean cloths or cotton balls (Q-Tip swabs) ;
   c. Carbon paper cut 3"x4" (from a citation) ;
   d. Wide scotch tape, transparent type (fingerprint kit) ;
   e. White cards, 3"x5" (rights card; F.I. card; fingerprint kit) .

2. Making the "Lift"
   a. Clean the surface thoroughly where the numbers are located with solvent and cloth. Make sure no oil film remains on the surface of the metal;
   b. Allow the surface to dry;
   c. Wipe carbon paper across the surface several times, leaving a carbon film around the number;
   d. Lay strip of scotch tape evenly and carefully across the number, smoothing it over with a finger;
   e. Lift the tape carefully from one end and pull away smoothly;
   f. Transfer the lift to the white card, carefully, from one end;
   g. Mark and preserve this evidence as you would a latent print.

D. NOW, MAKE YOUR CASE! MAKE YOUR REPORT! COMPLETE YOUR INVESTIGATION!

TRAINING BULLETIN #130

SUBJECT: WORDS AND PHRASES OF POLICE VERNAC-
ULAR—"In the Jug"

SOURCE: *Newsletter,* Davis Publishing Co., July 1971

PURPOSE: ROLL CALL TRAINING

AUTHOR: TRAINING DIVISION, STEEN #23, 7-19-71

Introduction:

Every Profession, Association, Country, Race, and Religion
forms and adopts words which are peculiar or unique to their
society. These words and phrases frequently then become ab-
breviated and esoteric and thus the vernacular of that society.
The origins of the words, through this devolution, then often
become lost.

The mark of the student of the craft which he claims as a profession is a familiarity with such of his origins.

"In the Jug"

Daily, Police Officers put people "in the jug." People "make
the bucket."

Long ago, Scottish Lords punished offenders against their
orders by placing them in iron yokes and then exhibited them
in public places. This yoke was known as the "joug."

Stone jails became known as "stone jougs."

In the course of time, the word became shortened to "jug"
and the word came to mean any place of confinement.

TRAINING BULLETIN #131

SUBJECT: EVIDENCE, DISPOSITION, CHARRED CUR-
RENCY AND GOVERNMENT BONDS

SOURCE: *Newsletter,* Davis Publishing Co., July 1971

PURPOSE: ROLL CALL TRAINING

AUTHOR: TRAINING DIVISION, STEEN #23, 7-19-71

Introduction:

Occasionally, and particularly with safe burglaries and at-
tempts, the contents of the safe, including currency and government bonds, will become burned and charred.

On these occasions, when the property is no longer needed
for investigation and Court presentation, and when the property is returned to the owner, the question of restoration and
restitution is raised.

Disposition of Charred Currency and Government Bonds:

Charred Currency—should be submitted to the currency Re-
demption Division, Office of the Treasurer of the U.S.,
Dept. of the Treasury, Washington, D.C.

Charred Government Bonds—should be sent to the Division of
Loans and Currency, Bureau of the Public Debt, Chicago,
Illinois.

TRAINING BULLETIN #132

SUBJECT: EVIDENCE, PRESERVATION, Protecting Metal from Corrosion

SOURCE: *Newsletter,* Davis Publishing Co., July 1971

PURPOSE: ROLL CALL TRAINING

AUTHOR: TRAINING DIVISION, STEEN #23, 7-19-71

Background:

Protecting metal surfaces from corrosion in humid areas has long been a problem.

A typical situation is present when it is desired to preserve a piece of metal showing tool impressions or striations.

Daly City and San Francisco frequently experience humidity of 70 to 80%. This is high humidity.

Solution:

It has been suggested that the placing of the metal in a bag, and enclosing a one inch cube of camphor may alleviate the problem.

There are also a number of rust and corrosion inhibitors available commercially, i.e. TSI-300, WD-40, etc. These products, however, may not be desireable, particularly when you are interested in paint, fluid, or petroleum based materials which also may be present on the tool or the piece of metal and are of evidentiary value.

TRAINING BULLETIN #136

TOPIC & COURSE

INSTRUCTOR	*DATE*	*DAY*	*TIME*	*NUMBER*	*HOURS*
BARRON, Sgt. J.	9-15-71	Wed.	0800-1700	Driver Training (12)	9
BARNER, Off. T.	9-28-71	Tue.	1340-1530	Warrants of Arrest and Search (17)	2
	9-10-71	Fri.	1340-1530	Narcotics (29)	2
	9-13-71	Mon.	1240-1410	Juveniles (33)	1½
	9-13-71	Mon.	1410-1530	Missing Persons (38.6)	1¹/₋
	9-14-71	Tue.	1340-1530	Sex Crimes (38.4)	2
BASTEDO, Det. L.	9-29-71	Wed.	1140-1230	Police Associations	1
	9-14-71	Tue.	1140-1330	Dead Bodies (31)	2
	9-16-71	Thur.	1340-1530	Auto Theft and Identification (38.5)	2
	9-20-71	Mon.	1230-1340	Thefts, Boosts, Pawn Shops (38.7)	1
	9-20-71	Mon.	1340-1530	Fictitious Paper and Credit Cards	2
CULLEY, Lt. T.	8-19-71	Thur.	1700-2000	The English Language (22)	3
	8-20-71	Fri.	1700-2000	Report Writing-Category Syst. (6c)	3
	8-26-71	Fri.	1700-2000	Report Writing-Category Syst. (6c)	3
	8-27-71	Fri.	1700-2000	Report Writing-Category Syst. (6c)	3
	8-30-71	Mon.	1900-2000	Station Security (20)	1
	8-30-71	Mon.	1700-1900	Family Disturbance Calls (36)	2
DORAN, Lt. J.	8-11-71	Wed.	1700-2000	Report Writing-	3
	8-12-71	Thur.	1700-2000	Theory of Reports (6a)	3
	8-13-71	Fri.	1700-2000	Memo Writing and Letter Writing (6b)	3
				The Category Report (6c)	
				The English Language (22)	
	8-6-71	Fri.	1700-2000	Interview and Interrogation— The Officer's Notebook; Note Taking; Questioning of Witnesses and Suspects (8a)	3
ETHERTON, Disp.	8-31-71	Tue.	1240-1530	Communications—Radio and TT (23)	3
FBI				Explosive Devices (27)	
GLASS, Off. A.	9-21-71	Tue.	1140-1330	Burglaries (38.3)	2
GUZMAN, Sgt. E.	8-10-71	Tue.	1140-1530	Arrests-Laws of Arrest, Search and Seizure; Mechanics of Arrest and Search (18a)	4
HANEBECK, Off. T.	9-17-71	Fri.	0800-1700	FIRST AID	9
HANSEN, Capt. D.	8-6-71	Fri.	1140-1430	Ethics, Discipline (7a)	3

INSTRUCTOR	DATE	DAY	TIME	TOPIC & COURSE NUMBER	HOURS
	8-16-71	Mon.	1140-1230	Human Relations-Talk to the People, the Press, etc. (26a)	1
	9-24-71	Fri.	1140-1230	A.S.T.	1
INGBRIGTSEN, Sgt.	9-30-71	Thur.	1140-1330	Municipal Code	2
JORDAN, Off. R.	8-4-71	Wed.	1140-1530	Defense Tactics	4
	8-9-71	Mon.	1140-1430	" "	3
	8-11-71	Wed.	1140-1430	" "	3
	8-16-71	Mon.	1240-1530	" "	3
	8-18-71	Wed.	1140-1430	" "	3
	8-23-71	Mon.	1240-1530	" "	3
	8-25-71	Wed.	1240-1530	" "	3
	8-30-71	Mon.	1240-1530	" "	3
	9-1-71	Wed.	1240-1530	" "	3
	9-27-71	Mon.	1240-1530	" "	3
	9-29-71	Wed.	1240-1530	" "	3
LA BRUZZO, Lt. P.	9-8-71	Wed.	1700-2200	Human Relations— Talk to the Races (26b)	5
MASCHINOT, Chas.	9-22-71	Wed.	1140-1530	Criminalistics-Crime Lab (34.1)	4
LYONS, Off. E.	8-6-71	Fri.	1440-1530	Ethics, Discipline, etc.— Appearance of the Officer (7b)	1
MERMON, M.	8-23-71	Mon.	1140-1230	Communications—Courtesy (24a)	1
	8-24-71	Tue.	1140-1230	Dictation (25)	1
PATROL III					83
II					30
POST				Riot and Disaster Procedures (32)	4
				Chemical Agents	8
				Range	8'
RECORDS	9-6-71	Mon.	0740-1610	Records and Communications	8
RICHARDSON, Off.	8-30-71	Mon.	1140-1230	Riot and Disaster Procedures—	1
	8-31-71	Tue.	1140-1230	Riots (32a)	1
SECRET SERVICE				Counterfeit Money	½
SEGUINE, Sgt. R.	9-7-71	Tue.	1140-1330	Vehicle Code (11)	2
	9-10-71	Fri.	1140-1330	" " (11)	2
	9-3-71	Fri.	1340-1530	A.B.C. (14)	2
	9-21-71	Tue.	1340-1530	Drunks and Drunk Drivers (16)	2
	8-17-71	Tue.	1140-1530	Accident Investigation (35)	4
SIMS, Capt. R.	9-29-71	Wed.	1140-1330	Evidence in Court (37)	2
SOLA, Off. R.	9-7-71	Tue.	1340-1530	Mentally Ill and Alcoholics (15)	2
	9-16-71	Thur.	1140-1330	Investigations—Robberies (38.1)	2

INSTRUCTOR	DATE	DAY	TIME	TOPIC & COURSE NUMBER	HOURS
STEEN, Off. S.	9-2-71	Thur.	1140-1330	Penal Code (9)	2
	9-3-71	Fri.	1140-1330	" " (9)	2
	8-24-71	Tue.	1340-1530	Jail Procedures (19)	2
	8-5-71	Thur.	1140-1530	Range Training—Weapons (5)	4
	8-9-71	Mon.	1430-1530	Range Training—Weapons (5)	1
	8-11-71	Wed.	1430-1530	Range Training—Weapons (5)	1
	8-18-71	Wed.	1430-1530	Range Training—Weapons (5)	1
TERRY, Lt. C.	9-2-71	Thur.	1340-1530	Detective Division (30)	2
	9-23-71	Thur.	1140-1230	Investigations— Investigator Assns. (38.8)	1
TRAINING DIV.	8-2-71	Mon.	1140-1530	Orientation (1)	4
	8-3-71	Tue.	1140-1530	Orientation (2)	4
	8-12-71	Thur.	1140-1200	Testing and Exams (40)	⅓
	8-13-71	Thur.	1140-1200	" " " (40)	⅓
	8-19-71	Thur.	1140-1200	" " " (40)	⅓
	8-20-71	Fri.	1140-1200	" " " (40)	⅓
	8-26-71	Thur.	1140-1200	" " " (40)	⅓
	8-27-71	Fri.	1140-1200	" " " (40)	⅓
	9-13-71	Mon.	1140-1230	" " " (40)	⅔
	9-30-71	Thur.	1340-1530	" " " (40)	2
	9-20-71	Mon.	1140-1230	" " " (40)	⅔
	9-27-71	Mon.	1140-1230	" " " (40)	⅔
	8-25-71	Wed.	1140-1230	Communications—Telephone Bomb Threats, Suicide Calls, etc. (24b)	1
	8-24-71	Tue.	1140-1330	Dictation (25)	2
WALSH, Capt, J.	9-16-71	Thur.	1700-1800	Interview and Interrogation Advising of Rights, etc. (8b)	1
	9-16-17	Thur.	1700-1800	Arrests—Citizen's Arrest (18b)	
	9-23-71	Thur.	1700-2000	Criminalistics-Lab (34.3)	3

INDEX

223